CONQUERING HEROES

CONQUERING HEROES

Elizabeth Phillips

THE BODLEY HEAD
LONDON

For Peter and Lulu

British Library Cataloguing
in Publication Data
Phillips, Elizabeth
Conquering heroes
I. Title
823'.914[F]   PR6066.H46/
ISBN 0–370–30873—5

© Elizabeth Phillips 1985
Phototypeset by Inforum Ltd, Portsmouth
Printed and bound in Great Britain for
The Bodley Head Ltd
9 Bow Street, London WC2E 7AL
by St Edmundsbury Press, Bury St Edmunds
First published 1985

CONQUERING HEROES

I
Nineteen forty-seven

They came across the crest of a hill in a ragged row: three scarecrow sisters etched angular and sharp against an early morning sky. They wore faded cotton frocks and scuffed brown sandals. The war was only just over and clothes were hard to come by.

Momentarily, they paused; ears, eyes, all senses stretched to test the path ahead. Then, reassured by the Summer silence, they moved on again, following the contour of the hill down towards the tank-trap. Here they fanned out, each finding the easiest crossing for her size.

'Don't go down on your bottom, Verity. You know what a mess it makes of your knickers,' Pauline snapped. She was the eldest, so she was used to giving orders. 'Honestly,' she added, 'you're so stupid.'

Verity had been making a backward, crouched descent, moving crabwise with her hands to balance her. Now, she lost concentration. Her heels slipped in the soft clay. Her legs involuntarily straightened and she slid down the rest of the bank, too surprised to even think of breaking her fall. She landed with a splash in the muddy trickle of water that ran along the bottom of the trap and sat for some moments gazing at the clumps of wild iris that swayed around her. Sunlight filtered through the translucent petals, dappling her skin with a soft yellow. Everything down here was yellow; the bank, the stream, even the husky clumps of bullrushes. Verity laughed and scooped up a handful of sparkling water, letting it run through her fingers in a cascade of rainbow drops.

'You loony!' Weener's shadow hovered above her for a

moment and then she was unceremoniously pulled to her feet. Weener was only a year older than Verity, but she was light years ahead of her in experience. She gathered the dripping skirt into a bunch and wrung a trickle of water from it. 'And look at your knickers,' she tutted. 'They're in a terrible state. Mummy'll kill us when we get home.'

Verity pulled her skirt higher while she craned her neck to inspect the damage. 'Perhaps we could wash them in the stream,' she suggested.

'How bad is it?' Pauline asked as she splashed towards them.

'Pretty bad. We were just wondering if we could wash them in the stream.' Weener's voice was deferential, but not without a certain nonchalance.

Pauline came closer, appraising Verity's mud-caked behind with the eye of experience. 'Probably better to leave them. It should just brush off when it dries. Come on,' she added airily and, with Weener bouncing behind her, she crossed the stream and started up the opposite bank.

Verity watched them for some moments through half-closed eyes. They were so much taller and so much more clever that sometimes her heart ached with the unfairness of it all. They were both pretty too. Pauline's face was a perfect oval. Her nose was short and straight, her mouth a prim little rosebud. She had round, green eyes with heavy, dark lashes which made them surprising and beautiful. Weener's eyes were grey and slanting. Her mouth was wide and always ready to break into a laugh. But, although they were so unalike, they had one thing in common which filled Verity with undying envy; their hair grew properly, so that it could be plaited. Watching those heavy brown plaits bouncing on her sisters' shoulders always filled Verity with sadness. 'Old Haystack', 'Old Wobble Nose', 'Old Bald Face', were just some of the names the other children called Verity, and she hated it because they were true. Her hair was fair and so light and curly that it never needed tying. Her nose had a knobble at the end which wobbled when she

2

talked and, as yet, she had not managed to grow any proper eyebrows or eyelashes. She was six now, so she supposed she never would. Pauline and Weener belonged together. Verity, the newcomer, was invariably in the way, but it was a fact she fought with rugged obstinacy.

'Bit of luck we left our socks off today,' she called after them, then wished for the thousandth time that she did not lisp quite so thickly. But they did not turn to tease her. All concentration was needed to climb the treacherous clay wall. Verity, watching their skilful brown limbs, felt a pang of inferiority. 'It *was* a bit of luck, though,' she told them mutinously as she splashed through the stream. 'My goodness, they'd have been absolutely ruined.'

Pauline reached the top, then turned and sighed audibly. 'That's why I told you to leave them off, stupid. Oh, for heaven's sake, Weener, you'd better give her a hand.'

Weener slithered back down the bank and Verity grabbed the extended hand, grateful for the warm, brown fingers that locked so neatly around her own. 'Bit bossy today, aren't we?' Weener whispered, and they both giggled at the private joke.

'Where are we going, then?' Weener asked when they had joined Pauline at the top.

'The haunted house,' Pauline replied, frowning with the importance of it all.

'Woooo!' Weener threw her arms around Verity and they both shook with mock terror, knocking their bony knees together as they chorused, 'Woo! Woo! The haunted house!' Pauline ignored them, stomping forward with such resolution that they stopped playing and ran to catch her up.

Now that they were in the heart of forbidden territory, the tension between them began to relax. They were still alert, still careful to keep together, but they had lost that animal sensitivity which had made them into a defensive unit.

So few people ever ventured beyond the tank-traps that the grass was waist high on Pauline and almost up to Verity's shoulders. Somewhere, far away, a yellow-hammer

3

stammered its demand for a little bit of bread and no cheese. The song was counterpointed by a calling lark, who soared like a black speck in the empty sky. Grasshoppers tickled their legs while bright blue butterflies danced indiscriminately with meadow-browns and cabbage-whites.

'This was once the lawn,' Pauline said, and the others nodded in solemn agreement. 'Poor Mr Rose,' she continued the litany in a clear sing-song voice, 'not for him the comfort of a happy marriage with the bride of his choice.'

'Oh dear me, no!' Weener the acolyte chimed in. 'But his faithful heart was true even unto death and it was death that got him in the end.'

'What did he die of?' Verity asked.

'Of love, stupid. Honestly, I told you that the last time we were here.' The grass around Pauline swayed with indignation. 'The house crumbled around him while his beautiful gardens ran wild and were choked with weeds.'

'But what did they do with him?' Verity's forehead crinkled with bewilderment.

'What do you mean, "what did they do with him"?'

'Well, I mean, did they come and bury him or something — after he had died?'

'Of course they did.'

'Then why didn't *they* mend the walls and pull up all the weeds?'

Pauline stopped and glared at her youngest sister. 'I hate you,' she snapped. 'I really do. I mean, who do you think you are, with your stupid questions?'

'I expect,' Weener said quickly and tactfully, 'I expect that nobody knew he was dead, so his body crumbled and mouldered in the house until there was nothing left but his broken heart, which rolled away and dropped with a plop between the floor boards.'

Pauline looked at her with genuine admiration. 'You could well be right, Weener. And that,' her voice assumed the sing-song tone again, 'is why his ghost walks these lonely and forgotten lands.' Weener smiled smugly and, as they

4

both looked so pleased with themselves, Verity dared another question. 'And were all the dirty men his friends?'

'No, of course they weren't,' Weener said quickly.

'Well, what are they doing here, then?'

'Oh, they just come here so they can be dirty in private and you'd better shut up, Verity. We'll be in the orchard soon and one of them might hear you.'

Instinctively, Verity drew nearer. Weener took her hand and smiled the special smile that made Verity love her so much. Together, they climbed over the crumbling bricks of the ruined wall, then plunged into the dappled green light of the orchard.

The fruit trees were old and their gnarled, black branches had intertwined to make a canopy of leaves. Brambles had formed impenetrable barriers between the trunks, climbed to the very top of the canopy, then dropped back towards the earth again. Now, their tendrils hung low enough to pluck the children by the hair.

Weener and Verity hurried down the rabbit-track Pauline had taken. This was the worst place for dirty men and it was important they should all stick together. They did not speak in that cathedral gloom. They simply hurried on, mindless of the snatching brambles and the little pricks of blood oozing from the scratches on their skin. It was a dismal place, full of muffled silence, but at last the green tunnel ended abruptly, pitching them into the brilliant light and tangled weeds of the old herb garden.

Still in silence and without looking back, Pauline led the way through a forest of wild raspberry canes, across weed-choked flowerbeds and then stopped dead on the mosaic floor which was all that was left of Mr Rose's house. 'So, here we are,' she told them factually.

'Will you tell us now?' Weener asked.

Pauline looked down at her hands and bit her lip. 'We're going abroad.' Her voice was flat and expressionless. 'This time we really are. I heard Mummy on the phone last night. She said that Daddy's settled at last and he's got it all fixed up. She's going to tell us today, but I thought I'd better break it to you first.'

'It'll probably be exciting,' Weener said, after a pause. 'Yes, I suppose so.'

'I don't want to go.' Verity's voice was flat and decisive. 'Why ever not?'

Verity squinted up at the sun while she ground her foot into Mr Rose's mosaic floor. 'Suppose —' her mind fumbled with the slender facts of her limited experience. 'Suppose —'

When Verity was three, she had a birthday party. It was a beautiful day because her birthday was in June. All the children came and there were jellies and trifles on a table in the back garden. Everyone was playing when the sirens sounded: the mournful scream ripped the heart out of their fun and made everyone stand still while the goosepimples rose upon their arms. 'Oh dear,' her mother's voice was expressionless. 'I suppose we'd better have the rest of our party indoors.'

'But it's day-time, Mummy,' Verity pleaded. 'It's all right in the day-time.'

'It'll be just as much fun indoors. Come on everybody. Help me with the plates. We don't want our jellies with bombs in them.'

They laughed as they dutifully obeyed and, much sooner than anybody had expected, the first thumps began to come. The children herded into the Anderson shelter, forming a square around the edge, with the jellies and the trifles in the middle.

Very soon the sky was grey with smoke, which was slashed through with orange flashes. Verity was watching them when she saw Caroline, her very best friend, chugging up the garden path. The short, fat legs were going like pistons and the purple face was shiny with mucus and tears. It was such an incongruous sight that at first she did not believe in it, but when she looked around the shelter, Caroline was not there.

'Mummy, Mummy! Caroline's running away!'

Her mother had been fixing the front of the shelter. Now, she turned just as Caroline reached the front gate and headed off down the road that led to the fields. 'Don't any of you dare to leave the shelter,' she said in such a terrifying voice that they all cowered back and shook their heads.

There was a tremendous thump which shook the house so forcibly that her mother swayed in front of them. And then, incredibly, she was gone.

Outside, the Germans were burning the sky and the golden afternoon had turned to lurid orange. Verity saw her mother running through the smoke, chasing the wretched Caroline who had long since disappeared.

Nobody cried; nobody screamed. There was such an enormous scream coming from the world around them that their terror seemed puny beside it. They sat. They watched. They waited. And, while time hung in limbo, Verity experienced real fear for the first time in her life.

She could not remember any more about the party except her anger when her mother got back with the wretched Caroline whimpering in her arms.

All the Pringles died that night. A doodlebug hit their shelter and spattered them around the walls. That was because they lived so close to the railway station which handled the supplies for Biggin Hill.

Verity's mother had not died and neither had Caroline, but suppose —

'Suppose —' she said now in answer to her sister's question, 'suppose another war should come. If we were all in abroad, we could quite easily get lost.' She was mortified to hear how thick her voice sounded.

The others squinted at her for some time and then Pauline, who had gone white beneath her tan, said casually, 'I'm going to pick some raspberries.'

Weener squeezed Verity's shoulder. 'Don't worry,' her voice was confident and reassuring. 'I'm nearly eight now,

7

you know, and I'm pretty clued up. I'll take care of you.'

A lump of gratitude rose in Verity's throat and she nuzzled her sister's armpit.

'God!' Pauline flung the words over her shoulder, 'you two are worse than a couple of lovers.'

Weener and Verity sprang apart with embarrassment and made their separate ways to the raspberry-canes.

The scent of the fruit was intoxicating; the taste delicate and warm. They browsed for some moments in silence, cramming their mouths and brushing away the little white moths that fluttered against their faces.

'I'm going to pick some for Mummy,' Verity called.

'Don't you dare!' Pauline shouted back.

'Why not?'

'She'll know we've been here, stupid.'

'I will, though,' Verity muttered mutinously. She picked a handful and pushed them into the little pocket on the leg of her bloomers. She felt it would be horribly mean not to share anything so delicious. She started to pick another handful, so absorbed in what she was doing, that she did not notice Weener until she bumped into her. Weener was moving stealthily backwards, her finger pressed to her lips.

'What is it?' Verity whispered.

'Dirty man.'

'Where?' Verity had never seen a dirty man, but Weener would not let her stay to look. Catching her by the wrist, she pulled her through the canes.

'Pauline,' Weener hissed.

Pauline straightened up, her eyes alive with question.

'Dirty man,' Verity told her importantly.

Pauline dropped the raspberries she had been holding. 'Run, girls!' she shouted, grabbing Weener's outstretched hand.

Suddenly, they were running; gasping, stumbling, ducking through the orchard, across the meadow and down into the tank-trap. They did not stop to look back as they scrambled up the bank. In fact, they did not stop running until they reached the red bars and none of them felt safe until they had squeezed through the barrier to the village green.

'Phew!' Pauline rolled her back against the paling. 'That was a close one! Right, Vety, let's have a look at your drawers.'

'I never saw him,' Verity muttered at she tugged at her skirt. 'I never see any dirty men. It isn't fair.'

Pauline did not answer as she concentrated on beating the crust of mud to the ground. 'There you are. I said it would all brush off.'

'Ow!' Verity twisted round, revealing the stain of crushed raspberries in her bloomer pocket.

Pauline looked at it for a moment, while her face clotted with anger. 'You filthy little pig!' she shouted. 'You've been stashing raspberries up your knickers! Well, that does it. You can do your own explaining to Mummy. I wash my hands of you,' and she stomped off across the green without looking back.

'Did you really see him?' Verity asked as she and Weener wandered home. Weener shrugged and nodded.

'I wish I could see interesting things,' Verity said wistfully.

'Perhaps you will when you're bigger.' Suddenly Weener stopped and grabbed Verity's hand. 'Oh, Vety,' she said urgently. 'I love it behind the red bars, don't you? Wouldn't it be lovely if we could live there — just you and me?'

'We could eat raspberries and you could make scones —'

'Vety,' Weener interrupted, 'she wouldn't really, would she — she won't really tell us that she's taking us abroad — she won't, will she, Vety?'

But she did. That afternoon, standing by the window with the sun behind her, she told them all just that. There was a certain excitement in the twist of her long fingered hands and she was smiling. 'We're going abroad,' she said. 'Won't that be lovely?'

'I don't want to go to abroad, thank you, Mummy.'

9

Verity tugged at her mother's skirt. 'I don't, honestly, Mummy. Honestly I don't.'

Her mother bent down and touched her face. 'Darling, you know I hate you doing that. And it's not *to* abroad. Abroad is only a name for all the countries that aren't England.'

'Which country are we going to then?' Pauline asked in a tight little voice.

'Well, to Germany, actually.'

Verity tugged more urgently at her mother's skirt. 'Is that where Germans come from?'

Suddenly their mother was a part of their group, kneeling down and hugging all of them. 'The war's over, silly goose. And now we're going to be with Daddy. It'll be lovely. Just you wait and see.'

They let her kiss them. None of them had the heart to spoil her excitement, but that night, as they got ready for bed, Pauline gave voice to what each of them was thinking. 'It's lunacy,' she muttered as she pulled on her pyjamas, 'sheer lunacy! And it's all Daddy's fault. Honestly, that man has been nothing but trouble since the day he stopped fighting in the war.'

II
The boat

Weener had never guessed it would happen like that. So many months had passed since they first heard about going abroad that she had begun to hope it would never happen. Bonfire night, her birthday and even Christmas had come and gone. There had been moments of high activity when trunks were packed, but they had soon been unpacked again. So the last flutter of excitement had left her unmoved. She had been able to smile knowingly at the grown-ups who kept telling her how thrilling it would be. She did not even believe it when they stepped on the train. Yet, here they were at Harwich and, far from being exciting, everything was flat and grey.

The February afternoon was dying. Quite undramatically, the leaden sky was closing into darkness above a sombre sea. Weener had never seen the sea before and, after a brief glance, she made up her mind that she never wanted to see it again. It was just a heaving stretch of someone else's scummy bathwater, endlessly slapping around the boat that was to take them away from home. A handful of discarded orange peel bobbed around the metal prow, drawn to it as if by magnetism. It was the only colour in that empty greyness, yet somehow the brightness of it was repellent. Weener shuddered and turned away. She always had hated oranges, she decided.

A woman was waiting for them in a wooden shed by the quayside. As they trouped in, she looked up, the brightness of her smile vying with the fly-blown electric light bulb that shone above her desk.

'Come in. Come in,' she almost sang as they shuffled

towards her. 'Right,' her voice was lower now, but it was kind. You could tell she liked children. 'We'll start with the biggest first, shall we? What's your name, dear?'

'Pauline Patricia Edwards,' Pauline answered clearly. 'We're going to Germany to see my Daddy.'

'Won't that be lovely!' the woman exclaimed, writing busily on a luggage-label in front of her. She tied the label to the top button of Pauline's coat. 'There, now you won't get lost, will you, Pauline Patricia?' She turned to Weener. 'Now you, dear.' Weener felt suddenly foolish. Her tongue was very large in her dry mouth, which was probably why her voice sounded so extraordinary as she whispered, 'Weener.'

The woman laughed. 'My goodness! How do you spell it?' Weener blushed, instinctively groping for Verity's hand. Verity moved closer and, as Weener stole a sideways look, she saw that she was glaring at the woman.

'Weener's only a nickname,' Pauline told the woman firmly. 'Her real name is Doreen Dianna Edwards. We only call her Weener in case she gets muddled up with me.'

'I see,' the woman replied solemnly. She wrote out the label and tied it to Weener's coat. 'Now,' she said brightly, 'last, but by no means least —?'

Weener nudged Verity. 'Tell her your name,' she whispered. Verity snatched her hand away and pushed it into her coat pocket. Weener turned to her in surprise and saw that Verity's forehead was drawn into an incongruous scowl. Her eyes, dark beneath it, were blazing straight at the woman.

'I must know your name, or otherwise I can't write out your label,' the woman said after some moments.

'I am not a thuitcathe!' Verity's lisp was somehow more accentuated by the darkness of her voice.

The woman laughed almost prettily and Weener was convulsed with giggles. Only Pauline stayed calm. 'Oh, for heaven's sake,' she said irritably. 'Her name's Verity. Honestly Verity, you're so stupid!'

The woman wrote out the label and tied it to Verity's coat. 'You must wear it, dear,' she murmured. 'We can't have you getting lost.'

Their mother came in. 'All done now, Mrs Edwards,' the woman told her as she thumbed through the papers on her desk. 'Nothing to stop you going aboard.'

Outside, on the quay, Verity tore the label from her coat and threw it at the scummy water. The string trailed limply as it missed its target by at least a foot. Verity ran after it and kicked it into the sea. Weener sighed. It was such a stupid thing to do, particularly as Verity was the only one who was really worried about getting lost. 'Oh well, I suppose I'll just have to look after you all the way to Germany,' she said, then turned away, wishing she had not taken on the responsibility. Verity shrugged and ran towards the boat.

Somebody had turned the lights on while they were in the shed and the huge, grey hull was now studded with golden circles. It looked warmer and more welcoming, but as Weener started up the gangway, a prickle of fear ran down her spine. She had expected a wooden boat with billowing canvas sails. This one was metal and you could see where the plates had been bolted together. For all she knew, it could be a warship.

The gangway moved uncertainly. Its angle was impossibly steep and the handrail was too high for her to reach. Verity and Pauline could manage because they had their mother to help them. It was often like that, Weener reflected. Youngest and eldest children seemed to have a call, almost a special right over a mother. Sometimes Weener dawdled behind just to see what would happen; just to find out if middle children were always left out.

As if in response to Weener's thoughts, her mother turned. 'Oh Weener!' she called. 'Poor darling. Wait there a moment.' She hurried Pauline and Verity up the last bit of the gangway, then came back and reached out her hand. Weener took it, warm with the knowledge that she had scored a point. For these brief moments, her mother was exclusively her own, while Verity and Pauline were left hanging around on the deck. She skipped over the nearest foot grip and the boards bounced under her feet.

'Isn't this exciting?' her mother asked.

'It's a bit springy,' Weener conceded and they both laughed.

The deck was surprisingly firm under their feet as they hurried across it. At the bottom of a flight of stairs, there was a cream-coloured corridor which led to their cabin.

'Well now,' their mother said when they had settled in, 'who wants to go on deck?' She made it sound a very tantalizing proposition.

'No thank you, Mummy,' Verity said and then began to undress with solemn concentration.

'You don't have to go to bed, Verity. She doesn't, does she, Mummy?' Weener asked anxiously.

'Not unless she wants to.'

Verity undressed to her underclothes, then looked around abstractedly for some pyjamas. Finding none, she climbed into the nearest bunk and pulled the thin covers up to her ears. 'That's right, poppet,' her mother said, kissing the unresponsive head. 'You have a sleep.' She turned to the others. 'Let's see if we can find a stewardess to keep an eye on her while we go up on deck.'

Weener was torn. Last night, in the darkness, she had promised Verity faithfully and faithfully that she would never leave her or let her get lost abroad. If Verity really was asleep, then to go on deck would not mean breaking that promise; she could hardly get lost if she was asleep in a bunk. But Weener was sure her sister was only pretending. Nobody could go to sleep just like that; not just when everything was getting exciting. She decided Verity must be planning something, so she yawned ostentatiously and murmured, 'Actually, I'm a bit tired too, Mummy,' then luxuriated in the comfort of being tucked into the other bottom bunk.

She closed her eyes and listened until the cabin door closed. 'You're not really asleep, are you, Verity?' she said as soon as they were alone. There was no reply so Weener got up and crossed the little bit of floor to look into her sister's face. 'You're not, Verity, are you?'

Verity shifted and muttered into her pillow.

'Are you awake?' Weener demanded. The eyelids fluttered and then Verity's head disappeared under the bedclothes.

Weener padded back to her bunk and sat looking down at her socks. She felt miserably cheated. Half of her wanted to shake Verity awake while the other half was resigned to the fact that neither of them knew their way to the deck. If they tried to find it alone, they probably would get lost and then it would all be her fault. She lay back on the bunk and closed her eyes.

The boat let out a long mournful moan that seemed to ache down to the marrow of her bones. There was a lurch; a churning, grinding feeling and then they began to move.

Weener jumped up, scrambled to the top bunk and peered through the porthole at the water below. It was quite dark now and the sea had changed from grey to black. It looked dangerous down there with the lights glittering on the swirling eddies which moved endlessly across each other's tracks.

'Just as well you didn't go on deck,' said a man's voice in her mind.

Weener recognised the voice and gasped with pleasure. She screwed her eyes up very tightly and hugged herself as hard as she could. 'I didn't know you were coming too, Dreamer,' she whispered. 'Have you brought your scallywags with you?'

'Got 'em tied up outside, old girl. Glad to see me then, are you?'

Weener nodded. 'I never thought you'd come all the way to Germany with me. Do you think Daddy'll mind?'

'Well, he's not your father really, is he Doreen? He's Verity's stupid Daddy. Now, hop into bed and I'll think up a really good dream for you.'

Weener obeyed, keeping her eyes tightly closed so she would be able to see him. She loved looking at her Dreamer. It gave her a special excitement to know he would terrify the others if they could only see him: his hair was so thick and long and his eyes burned like two bright coals in a fire. He was smiling now, his sharp teeth biting down on his lower lip. 'Red, white and blue,' he sang in her brain, 'you dirty kangaroo. I know what you did behind the dining-room curtains.'

Weener laughed quietly. 'Well, you made me, Dreamer, so it's your fault, isn't it; not mine,' and then she fell asleep.

III
Eva

Abroad was every bit as terrible as Verity had expected. After the boat, they spent the night on swaying trains that lurched and rattled them deeper into the heart of foreign territory.

At each main station, their mother bought them all a cup of tea. They had to be careful to save the dregs so that she could throw them out of the window while the train was going. The groundy liquid clung to the glass and looked like vomit against the reflected, sleep-denying light. From time to time, the carriage door opened and fellow travellers threatened their privacy. Seeing the state of the window and the weary children, they quicky bobbed back to the corridor, muttering a string of foreign words before carefully closing the door.

At one station, they all got out and went to look for their father, but he was not there. They waited while the station emptied and the loudspeaker boomed hollow, unintelligible messages. Their mother went to the telephone and, while she was away, a dry wind blew dusty gusts up their skirts which froze the tops of their legs. They were all too tired, too cold and too depressed to be afraid. They stood in a row by the platform, holding hands, waiting for their mother to remove them from that vast confusing place.

'Daddy's been posted,' she told them when she got back. 'We're going to go just a bit further on our own, I'm afraid.'

Verity did not blame her father for not meeting them. In fact, she felt it was unreasonable to expect him to know where they would be. She had already begun to grasp the enormous, flat emptiness that made up abroad. She hoped they would eventually find him, though. She had only met him once and that was two years ago, when she was four. But she had formed a special personal attachment to him, mainly because they looked so alike.

During the war, Weener had convinced her sisters that they all had different fathers. Pauline's was as tall as an oak tree, and was very dark. Weener's was as tall as the house and had long, curly brown hair. But Verity's father, according to the myth, was only as tall as the doorway. His hair was short, yellow and curly, just like Verity's.

On that day when their father visited them, they were all agog to see which one it would be. To Pauline and Weener's bitter disappointment, it was Verity's father who turned up. He stayed with them for a little while and taught them to make houses out of long grass. He gave them Turkish delight which made them sick and he told long stories about the war which anyone could see were not true. Verity adored him, but the others hung back until one day, when they were all in the garden together, he asked them why.

'Weener and I are very fond of you,' Pauline told him. 'But we want our own fathers, you see. I mean it's hardly fair to expect us to make do with Verity's Daddy, now is it?'

To everyone's surprise, he began to laugh. He laughed so much that his face went mauve and then he broke it to Pauline and Weener that he was their father too. It was a bitter disappointment to them. He looked so like Verity who, as they often told her, was very peculiar. Even now, it made Verity smile because the one thing that all grown-ups seemed to be agreed on was that her father was good looking. Right at the outset of their journey, she had decided that if they ever did find him in Germany, she would stretch her arms around him and hold him very tight while she said, 'I love you very much, Daddy, because you're such a handsome man.'

But the journey was so long and confusing and it was so late when they finally spotted him, waiting for them on a funny little platform, that Verity found she had gone off him to such an extent that even the sight of his camel-hair coat and army hat gave her no pleasure at all. She pretended to go to sleep in the car and when he carried her into the tall building which was to be their new home, she did not cuddle against him at all. He kissed her forehead with his cold, bristly moustache.

'I'm sorry I wasn't there to meet you,' he whispered the message specially to her, 'but I do love you all very much, monkey.' Verity did not stir because she did not believe him.

When she woke the next morning, she had no recollection of being put to bed, but she knew instantly where she was. The pillow and mattress were as hard as iron: no English bed could ever be so uncomfortable. Pauline and Weener were asleep and both were totally unresponsive. Verity padded over to the window and put her head under the curtains so that she could look out.

The sky was a breathtaking, brittle blue. The window looked down on to a clump of pine trees with patches of sparkling snow between them. A soldier was walking very slowly backwards and forwards, the sun glinting on the barrel of his rifle. Verity waved to him, but he did not wave back.

Suddenly she realized that, more than anything in the world, she needed to find a lavatory. Without stopping to dress, she padded out of the bedroom and found herself in a long, brown corridor. There were doors leading off it, but Verity had no way of knowing what was behind them. Eventually, she decided the only way to find out was to open one of them. The doorknob was bright, shiny brass and it moved easily beneath her hand. The door swung open noiselessly, revealing a lady with a huge pink bottom, standing in naked contemplation before her mirror.

'Excuse me —' Verity began and then was so overcome by giggles that she could not spit the message out.

The lady turned and marched towards the doorway. Her

19

breasts wagged angrily, which made her even funnier to look at. She pushed Verity back across the threshold without a word, then slammed the door in her face.

Verity's giggles were drowned by a sickening tide of fear and she ran blindly down the rest of the corridor. She found a flight of stairs and stumbled down them, then followed another darker corridor only to discover that it ended abruptly in two green doors. She was now so lost that there was no hope of finding her bedroom again. Timidly she pushed the doors in front of her and found that they swung effortlessly from the slight pressure of her fingers. She sidled through and found herself in an enormous, tiled kitchen, which glittered with sunlight and cleanliness. A group of red-faced women were working with such feverish intensity that none of them noticed her.

Verity walked up to the nearest one and tugged at the hem of her apron. 'Excuse me,' she said. The woman paused and then looked down in blank astonishment. 'Could you tell me where the lavatory is, please?' Verity asked in her most seriously polite voice.

The woman let out a gasp of real pleasure as she swooped down and gathered Verity in her arms, then she stood up holding her very tightly against the mound of squashy fat that was her bosom. Verity's bladder shook dangerously. 'Please,' she implored the woman, 'I must find the lavatory.'

The woman began to smother her in suffocating kisses, then stopped to shout some words of German to her companions. They crowded round, gasping and exclaiming. They examined Verity's hands and feet. They stroked her hair, stretching it out as far as it would go, then letting it snap back into curls again. They took it in turns to snatch her from one another's arms, squealing with delight and pretending to run away with her. Although Verity could not understand what they were saying, she gathered it was all complimentary and she began to enjoy the game, momentarily forgetting her pressing need.

'Oh, let me,' a voice said from the doorway. The women

20

stopped playing, giving Verity a chance to see who it was who had spoken in English.

A tall girl with a round, florid face and frizzy yellow hair had come into the room. She was wearing a cheap black dress with a starched white apron over it. When she moved, her body quivered like a jelly because she was so plump.

'Are you English?' Verity asked.

'No, but a few words I am speaking so I am a clever little German, yes?' She spoke rapidly to the other women in their own language and Verity was passed into her arms. 'You are of Captain Edwards' family, no?' she said as she carried Verity over to the fireplace. Verity shook her head.

'Oh yes, I think. Last night I see you with him.' The girl sat down, setting Verity on her knee as she did so. 'What is the name of your father?'

'Daddy,' Verity said, and an ominous trickle wetted the tops of her legs. She wriggled against it and the girl laughed. 'Ah!' she said. 'So now I am seeing.' She stood up and carried Verity out of the room. Verity shut her eyes tightly and prayed she would not wet herself. When she opened them again, she and the girl were in a room which housed both a lavatory and a wash-basin.

'I can manage on my own,' Verity said firmly, but the girl did not seem to understand.

'I am Eva,' she said as she rolled down Verity's pyjama trousers and plonked her onto the pan. 'You see how nicely I do for you. I speak to the mother today, yes? Maybe she is letting me your nanny be.'

IV
Kaputzel

Of all Verity's sins, Pauline decided, the most unforgiveable was her introduction of Eva to the family. If only Verity had not gone out of the servants' entrance that first morning, she would never have made her way to the kitchen or found a nursemaid for them. Pauline suspected that she had only been looking for an audience. There were two perfectly adequate lavatories in their quarters.

It was, in fact, a very comfortable flat, or it would be if Eva were not living there too. There was a nursery, a large living-room, two bathrooms and three bedrooms. If only Eva had not been their nursemaid, that would have meant one bedroom for her parents, one for her two sisters and one for her. As it was, Eva had the third room, which meant that Pauline had to share with the other two.

She had never shared a room with her sisters before and she found it very objectionable. Weener muttered all through the night and Verity snored. When Pauline told her parents that she was not getting a wink of sleep, her mother simply laughed and pulled her pigtails while her father christened her, 'The Queen of Sheba.' Pauline would not have minded the nickname if it had not been used so derisively. Now, when her father met her, he would bow very deeply and say, 'Good day, your majesty,' and though Pauline glared back as coldly as she could, he was invariably convulsed with laughter. His behaviour was having a bad effect on the others, who seemed to have forgotten her position as the eldest and had begun to treat her with a total lack of deference.

Eva, of course, backed them up, but then, she would;

being so hateful and inferior. At first it had been quite easy to keep her in her place. She spoke such bad English that Pauline only had to demand that she should, 'longitude to latitude the curtains' to throw her into a state of tearful confusion. She was learning fast though, and now she had grasped the fact that Pauline had been intentionally confusing her, her dislike became obvious.

Pauline did not care if Eva hated her. She was, after all, only German and Pauline could always go out to avoid her. There was a pretty good playroom in the building with a lot of toys in it. During their first few weeks in Germany, Pauline had spent most of her time down there, building a Meccano crane with a boy called Robin. His parents had just been posted though, so now she had no one to play with. It was too cold to stay out for long, although she did sometimes take herself for a walk around the grounds. She was beginning to make friends with a German boy called Wolfgang, but it was a bit difficult to talk to him as he spoke no English and she could not speak German yet.

The house they were living in was called the Kaiserhof and, during the war, it had been used as a leave centre for German officers. When the English beat the Germans, they took the Kaiserhof over and used it as a leave centre for British officers and their families. It gave Pauline immense satisfaction to ponder on that.

There was a communal lounge and a large dining-room where people could eat if they were feeling too lonely to stay in their quarters. Pauline and her sisters had to eat in the nursery with Eva, which Pauline thought was very unfair. Just to show that she could if she wanted to, she liked to hang around the lounge and dining-room and chat to any grown-ups who were prepared to listen to her.

She was sitting on the window seat in the dining-room now, her legs against the scorching radiator grill and her nose pressed to the freezing window-pane. A new waiter was moving slowly but methodically round the tables. He was singing very quietly, the buzz of his voice growing louder and then receding as he made his way around the room.

'You're new here, aren't you?' Pauline asked, without turning from the window. He did not answer.

'What's that you're singing?' This time she treated him to one of her more searching glances. He was small and dark and there was something very jaunty about the twitch of his thick moustache.

'You like the song then, Fräulein?' he said without answering the question.

Pauline shrugged. 'Not particularly. I mean, you could hardly expect me to like a German song, now could you?' She saw dislike flicker in his eyes, but the carefully arranged smile did not leave his face.

'But it is an English song, Fräulein. Listen, I sing for you in English,' and he began to sing 'You Are My Sunshine' in an attractive, deep voice. Pauline blushed and he stopped singing and laughed. 'Now you recognize?'

'No,' she answered coldly and flipped her plaits back across her shoulders. 'Still, you did sing it very nicely. What's your name?'

'You can call me Fritz.'

'Is that your name?'

He shrugged and flipped a crumb from the nearest table-cloth.

'There's no point in me calling you Fritz, if it's not your name, now is there?'

'You may as well call me that. All the other English do.' Pauline nodded, realizing he felt degraded by it. 'Very well,' she said and turned her attention back to the window.

'But the Fräulein has not told me her name.'

'Pauline Edwards.'

'Do I call you Pauline, Miss Pauline or Miss Edwards?'

'Miss Pauline will do very well.'

She thought she heard him laugh again, but at that moment, her whole attention was taken by a gang of ragged dogs who came pelting round the side of the Kaiserhof and

24

began a fight on the snowy waste outside the dining-room window. The leader was a tall, balding red-setter who held a chunk of bread between his strong, yellow teeth. He was besieged by a pack of tangled spaniels, terriers and mongrels, while one black labrador, limping on deeply scarred legs, struggled to keep up.

'Who do all those awful dogs belong to?' Pauline asked.

Fritz came over to the window-seat and rested one knee on the cushion. 'Ah,' he said softly, 'so they are back.'

'Where have they been, then?'

'Hunting. From time to time they go off into the forest. For miles they go in search of food, but they always come back.'

'But who do they belong to?' Pauline demanded.

'To the English. The father thinks how nice to have a faithful dog to love and be part of the family. Then he gets posted. He cannot take the dog, so he leaves him behind. The Germans have no money: not food even for themselves. So the faithful dog starves. So kind to their animals, the English: them and the Americans.'

'I don't think that's kind,' Pauline said stoutly. 'I think it's terribly, terribly cruel.'

Fritz put an arm around her shoulder. 'Then you are not such a bad little girl, after all,' he said, and Pauline found herself smiling back at him.

Outside, a stocky little dog had broken away from the pack and was harassing the setter by darting backwards and forwards across his path. The setter's lips curled back in a snarl, but the little dog was not intimidated. He leapt in the air, wiggling his flanks to give him more height. The setter watched him, his head cocked to one side as he followed the little dog's rise and subsequent fall. He was clearly puzzled; so much so, that when the little dog jumped again, he was able to snatch the bread from the setter's slackened jaw and set off with it across the snow before the rest of the pack realized what had happened. 'Oh!' Pauline gasped. 'Oh, isn't he wonderful? What's his name, Fritz, do you know?'

'That one, he's called Kaputzel. He's a very clever little dog. Once a lorry ran over him and broke every bone in his body. That's why he's called Kaputzel. It means, "all broken up".'

Pauline sighed. 'I wish I could look after him.'

'So you can leave him behind when the father is posted?'

'No,' she said earnestly. 'No, I wouldn't. Honestly, Fritz.'

'Then go and take him.'

Pauline looked at him in surprise, then jumped down from the window seat.

'Here, Fräulein Päulein!' he shouted to her as she darted across the dining-room. She turned by the sliding doors and he tossed her a bread roll. 'You'd better take this. A German dog does all things for a crust of English bread.'

The roll dropped at her feet and she bobbed down quickly to pick it up. 'Thanks,' she shouted over her shoulder as she ran to the main entrance.

Outside, the cold hit her in the face, jangling her teeth and making her eyes stream with tears. The barking, baying and yapping of the pack was all the noise in the world.

'Kaputzel!' She strained her voice above the din. 'Here, Kaputzel! Here!'

The dogs tore to the shelter of a clump of pine trees and stood there at bay with hackles up. Pauline ran towards them, tearing a lump from the roll with trembling, numb fingers. 'Bread, Kaputzel,' she shouted as she threw the crumbs towards the dogs. 'Come on, Kaputzel!'

The pack wavered, then pressed forward. Slowly at first, but with a gathering and terrifying momentum, they bore down on the scattered crumbs, woolfed them, then rushed at Pauline demanding the rest of the roll. She held it above her head, oblivious of the threatening teeth.

'Not you!' she shouted fiercely at the moth-eaten setter. 'It's for Kaputzel. Where are you? Kaputzel!'

The little dog came slinking through the red-setter's legs. He was dachshund shaped but he was too tall to be a true breed. His fur was dirty white with brindle and pale brown

26

splodges. He smiled ingratiatingly, slinking forward with his belly scraping the snow.

Pauline broke off a piece of roll and held it enticingly just beyond his reach. 'Come on, Kaputzel,' she wheedled. The dog momentarily dropped its haunches, then sprang at her. He had thrown himself not at the morsel she had offered, but at the large chunk she was still holding above her head. Pauline tottered, made a wild grab at the dog and then slipped backwards on the frozen snow.

With a single yelp, the setter drove the pack straight towards her. As she fought to get up, Kaputzel snatched the bread from her hand and raced away with it towards the trees. The other dogs thundered over her prone body, their claws scratching her arms and legs and ripping a large hole in her skirt.

'So, Boadicea,' Fritz said as he helped her to her feet, 'the little German dog was too clever for you.'

Pauline looked up at him uncomprehendingly and, as she did so, his expression changed.

'*Raus*!' he shouted fiercely at the dogs. He shook his fist and glowered at them as they slunk round the corner of the building.

'Oh Fritz!'

Pauline turned in surprise and saw her mother hurrying towards them. 'Oh Fritz,' she gasped as she came nearer. 'Oh thank you. Thank you! I saw it from the window. Pauline, are you hurt? Whatever possessed you?'

Fritz bowed slightly and smiled knowingly. 'I think, perhaps, the Fräulein wanted a little dog to play with. If madam is in agreement, I will get a little dog, but not a wild one, eh?'

'I don't want any old dog. I want Kaputzel. Please, Mummy, please. He's been all broken up by a lorry and he's the best dog in the whole world.'

'Darling, look at the state of you!' Her mother knelt beside her and pressed a small, lace edged handkerchief to Pauline's torn knee. It was quickly saturated with blood.

'If madam would permit, I think perhaps the Fräulein should see the doctor to make sure the wounds are properly clean.'

'Yes, yes, of course, How silly of me.' She led the way towards the main entrance, Pauline and Fritz following a little way behind. Pauline paused and looked back at the churned-up snow and the trail of bright red blood spots leading straight up to her feet. Fritz squeezed her shoulder gently. 'Yes,' he said softly so that her mother could not hear. 'Boadicea is brave and she feels no pain, so she shall have a little dog, but not Kaputzel. Kaputzel is a German dog. He does not like the English.'

V
Wolfgang

Because Fritz had been so brave in saving Pauline from the wild dogs, he became a special favourite with their mother. Now, it was always Fritz who brought their meals up to them. He would come sailing into the nursery with their tray delicately balanced on his fingertips. Before opening the door, he would make a noise like a ship's fog-horn which always made Verity and Weener laugh. But, although he was kind to all of them, it was Pauline who was his favourite.

'Are you and Fritz lovers?' Weener asked one day after he had made a special fuss over serving Pauline's lunch.

'No, of course not!' Pauline snapped. 'Wolfgang's my lover. Honestly, Weener, sometimes you're as stupid as Verity.'

'I wish I could have a lover,' Weener sighed.

'You've got your Dreamer.'

'Yes, I suppose so. Does Wolfgang ever kiss you?'

'No, of course not. The things we do are much too important for you to understand.'

'What then?' Weener asked, more from boredom than any real interest.

'Well, he teaches me things like how to do owl hoots; throw knives; kill people. You know, important things like that.'

Weener breathed on the window and drew a pin man in the steam from her breath. 'You shouldn't kill people. It's very wicked and God will strike you dead.'

'No He won't. Sometimes it's necessary to kill people. You'll find out all about it when you're old enough.'

'No I won't!' Weener said hotly. 'How would you like it if people came and killed you?' She stood up and threatened Pauline with her face. 'If I ever catch you killing people, I'll tell Mummy, and Daddy too, so there!'

Pauline hit her hard round the ear. There had been no warning in her face and she moved so quickly that she caught Weener unprepared. Weener tottered backwards, cradling her stinging ear, then she let out an enormous bellow of pain and ran to tell Eva.

'Oh, for heaven's sake,' Pauline said irritably as she pulled on her coat. 'I'm going for a walk. Come on, Goldie.'

Goldie was a fat cocker-spaniel: the wonderful little dog that Fritz had promised her. He was old. He could not do tricks and he could not run. Still, he was better than nothing, Pauline supposed.

The other dogs had all gone off hunting again after the bread fiasco. Pauline often wondered if Fritz had tricked her into that. She had even asked him once, but he simply smiled and said, 'Now, why should I trick you, Fräulein? Who knows, the little dog might have taken to you and that would have been good for you both.'

Pauline wished it could have been Kaputzel following her down the service corridor. 'Oh, for heaven's sake, come on, Goldie.' She waited while the fat spaniel laboured to catch her up. He stopped beside her and sat down, rolling his vacant eyes and gasping for breath. Pauline grabbed him by the collar, then hurried him down the back stairs and out of the side entrance.

Wolfgang was waiting with his back against a tree. He whistled to Pauline and she ran over to meet him. He lolled round to look at her, his eyes cold and sneering. 'So, you come for me, ja?'

Pauline shrugged. 'The dog.' she said simply, then turned back to look at Goldie.

It was beginning to turn warmer and the snow was getting softer. Goldie's big feet floundered as he trundled towards them. Wolfgang scooped up a handful of snow, patted it into a ball, then threw it straight at the dog. It hit him full in the face and for a few moments he sat down staring blankly at them. Wolfgang shook with laughter and threw another snowball which hit Goldie's back. The dog stood up and pottered back to the Kaiserhof, shaking himself laboriously before going inside. Wolfgang punched Pauline's arm and she laughed dutifully.

'Why you and that fool?' he asked.

Pauline broke a twig from the nearest tree and drew in the snow with it. She drew pin caricatures of Verity and Weener with the dog between them, then wrote 'family fools' in wonky capitals beneath it. It took some moments for Wolfgang to understand. She spelt the letters out for him and he suddenly shouted with laughter and clouted her so hard round the shoulders that she reeled forward.

'You!' His clear voice hung in the air above them. 'You good enough to be boy!' He raced away over the snow. 'Come!' he shouted over his shoulder.

Wolfgang had a hut beside the river. It was a little wooden shack with a pine-log balcony. Pauline was glad when he led her there. He stood in the doorway, beckoning to her and she hurried to catch him up.

The hut smelt of snow and cold sacking. A pile of logs stood in one corner and Wolfgang reached behind it to pull out his knife. He took a turnip from one of the sacks and began to peel it, squatting on the bare boards. Pauline watched him in admiration. He had such a grown-up way of doing things. The knife was grown-up too: not the sort of penknife that the boys at home had, but a sensible, thick-bladed knife with a black, scored handle.

'Have you really killed grown-ups with that?' she asked. He looked at her blankly. She stood up and he followed her out onto the balcony. She drew a pin picture in the snow of a boy stabbing a man and Wolfgang studied it, then nodded.

'Oh yes,' he said calmly as he passed her a piece of raw turnip.

31

She took it and ate it slowly while she looked at him. He did not seem to be any older than she was and, if anything, he was a little bit shorter. She scratched the first picture out, then quickly drew a pin woman in the snow and wrote under it 'ME'.

Wolfgang looked at it, then smiled and pointed at her. 'You?'

Pauline nodded, then quickly wrote 10 under it. She drew a picture of Wolfgang with a big question-mark. He thought for a moment, then scratched 103 beneath it. Pauline pushed him in annoyance and he rolled onto his back, chewing on his piece of raw turnip and laughing up at the sky.

Pauline dusted her hands on her skirt. 'If you weren't so stupid,' she muttered as she wandered across the balcony, 'I wouldn't have to keep drawing pictures for you.'

He came up and tugged her by the sleeve. 'Not know,' he said simply. Pauline did not believe him so she shrugged away and began to saunter back towards the Kaiserhof. He did not follow even though she slowed her pace right down to give him a chance to catch up and apologize. She did not want to quarrel with him, but it was unthinkable that she should turn around and make it up. 'I've had just about enough of these people,' she muttered, pushing her hands deep into her pockets. 'It's high time they learned that I'm one English person they can't make a fool of.'

'Miss Pauline! Miss Pauline!' Eva's voice rang across the snow. Pauline smiled. So, the stupid woman had actually got off her bottom and come out to look for her. That was a turn-up for the books. She ducked into the clump of trees and hid behind the nearest trunk.

She could hear Eva quite close now, muttering angrily to herself in German. Pauline waited. As soon as Eva had passed, she planned to slip quietly round and walk into the Kaiserhof through the front entrance. It would give her at least half an hour's peace while Eva searched for her and by the time she gave up, the sting would have gone out of her anger. She might even be relieved to find that Pauline was safe.

The muttering and the footsteps were very close now. Pauline timed it by ear and, as Eva drew level, she quietly slipped to the other side of the tree. The footsteps and the muttering stopped. Pauline held her breath and flattened her back against the trunk. 'So you are behind the tree, eh?' Eva's voice was full of controlled nastiness. 'You think you can play games with Eva Königsberg? Yet you are so stupid you do not even think of the mark your feet make in the snow.'

Damn, Pauline thought. It was the strongest word in her vocabulary and she would have liked to shout it out at the top of her voice. However, this was neither the time nor the place. Her only hope now was to brazen it out. She began to walk slowly away. In her experience, people very rarely ran after a person who was walking.

'You think I cannot see you?' Eva shouted. It was half statement, half question. Pauline shrugged and went on walking. A few heavy, pounding footsteps brought Eva near enough to grab her savagely by the arm.

Pauline did not look up. 'Let go of my arm.' she said coolly. 'Let go at once.'

To her surprise, the vice-like grip was tightened and she found herself being propelled towards the side entrance.

Eva opened the door with her free hand. 'In!' she commanded.

'I beg your pardon!' Pauline made her voice cold and threatening. Eva pushed her through the doorway and, once they were both in the dingy little hallway, she whipped up Pauline's skirt and lashed two ringing slaps across the tops of her legs, on the gap between her stocking-tops and knickers.

'How dare you!' Pauline said with more shock and anger than she really felt.

'Dare? Oh yes I dare. You! You witch, I dare, do you hear?'

Pauline shrugged. 'Obviously I can hear as you're shout-ing it straight down my ear.' She looked away, struggling to keep her face impassive, although she *was* beginning to get a bit frightened. Eva had never played up like this. Eva caught hold of one of her plaits and jerked her head round and back.

'You look when I speak! You look!'

Her face was very close and, in that half-light, her eyes were black with anger. Pauline noticed there were little drops of sweat on her round, red forehead.

'I shall report this to my mother.' she said coolly.

Eva let go of her plait, grabbed her by both shoulders and shook her roughly. 'Report! Already I am reporting. I report how you lie about a good German boy. A German boy who fights for his fatherland before he is your age. Oh yes, he fights. In the streets he fights when others have given up. And you? You say to your sister you lovers with him!' She slapped Pauline across the face. 'He spits on you, you Jew! Now, for your lies he must go away; he, with no father and no mother. While you, you stay and you eat. You eat his bread. You take his home. You take all and you drive him away.' She leant her back against the wall and momentarily closed her eyes.

Pauline was relieved to find all this fuss had been about something so trivial. 'Oh don't be so stupid. Of course he's got a father and mother,' she said scornfully. 'And of course he hasn't got to go away. Really! What a lot of fuss about nothing.' She had expected another outburst, but instead, a tear gathered on her nursemaid's blunt, blonde eyelashes. She seemed to be unaware of it until it rolled down her cheek and then she brushed it aside with the back of her hand as if it were a thing of no consequence. She opened her eyes and stared briefly at the wall in front of her.

'You cold, witch, English child,' she said wearily. 'You know nothing; nothing at all.' She wandered along the short passageway, then stopped by the stairs. 'You come, please,' she said in her normal voice.

VI
Eva's letter

Verity was in the nursery, curled up in the wicker chair with Goldie in her arms. The dog's nose was buried in her hair and she was giggling and whispering into his ear.

'That's my dog,' Pauline said automatically as she walked through the door. Verity pulled Goldie closer and looked up defiantly.

'You threw snowballs at him.'

'I did not!'

'Yes you did. Eva saw you and she told Mummy and Mummy's furious.' Goldie began to struggle in her arms. She hung on for a few moments and then let him go. He thudded down to the floor and padded over to Pauline, wagging his ridiculous stump of a tail. Pauline patted him while she looked at her sister. The room was stuffily hot and Verity had the frowsty look of somebody who has been indoors too long.

'You ought to go out more,' Pauline said coldly. 'You're beginning to get as fat and stupid as Eva.' She took off her coat and threw it on the table.

Suddenly Eva was with them. 'You will pick that up, please, and hang in the bedroom.'

Pauline stared at her incredulously and then obeyed. She did not want a repetition of what had happened downstairs; particularly not with Verity there.

'Oh yes,' Eva said as Pauline came back into the nursery, 'I tell the mother. I tell how you are with me and your sisters: how they are little angels while you, you are a black witch from hell. Now things change. You see, Miss Pauline. You see how they change.'

35

Pauline shrugged. 'I shall go and speak to her myself and she's not "the mother". She's my mother, so there.' And she marched out of the nursery with Goldie waddling behind her.

She stomped down the short dark corridor that led to the drawing-room, then paused for a moment outside the door. She was hit by a wave of uncharacteristic uncertainty. Over the last few weeks, the whole family had begun to drift apart. Now Eva was there to cope with the day to day running of life, there was no excuse for the girls to go and bother their mother. They still saw a lot of her, of course, but that bond of survival dependency had been broken. Now, when they met, it was because their mother wished it. They had to be scrubbed and groomed for the occasion, which gave it a certain formality.

Their mother was changing too. In the old days, she had been so absent-minded that she was quite capable of going shopping with an old plastic comb still stuck in her hair. Now, she was always immaculate. An air of glamour hung around her, like an expensive perfume. In just a few weeks, she had become beautiful and unattainable.

Pauline lifted her fist to knock on the door, then shrugged back her uncertainty in a wave of rebellion. She's my mother, she told herself mutinously; I'm damn well not going to knock on the door as if she were the headmistress. She turned the knob and pushed the door open abruptly.

The room, with its pale blue shadows, was dominated by an open fire. Her father was standing with his back to the grate, the orange light making strange work of his huge frame and overpowering features. Pauline wavered and then began to close the door. There was something about her father that she found very intimidating. He was so very tall and, because of the war, she was unused to the company of men.

'Don't dawdle around there, Pauline,' he barked. 'Come in. Come here where I can see you.'

'No, no. It's quite all right, Daddy. I'll come back later.'
She kept her voice casual and was careful to stay in the
shadow of the half-closed door. Goldie pushed past her and
waddled over to the fireplace. He plumped himself down on
the hearth-rug and rolled his eyes ingratiatingly. Pauline felt
a wave of hatred for him.

'Come here, Goldie!' she shouted imperiously. The dog
wavered while her father's face darkened.

'I won't tell you twice, Pauline.' His voice had an edge of
discipline that made it impossible to disobey. She followed
Goldie into the room, carefully closing the door behind her.

'I've been getting some pretty alarming reports about you,
my girl,' he said, once she had joined him by the fire. Pauline
stared up at him, but did not reply. 'And you can take that
look off your face,' he went on. 'I won't stand for dumb
insolence. I've had Eva in here in fits of tears, threatening to
leave and goodness knows what else. I gather you've been
pretty beastly to everyone — even the poor old dog. Now,
what have you got to say for yourself?'

Wrongly supposing that he wanted an answer, Pauline
gave him one. 'If you ask me,' she said clearly and decisively,
'it would be a jolly good thing if Eva did leave. She's a liar
and a thief and she's having a very bad effect on Verity.'

'Oh, she is, is she?' the moustache twitched dangerously.

'Yes she is,' Pauline countered. 'Verity never wants to go
out now. She just slouches around our quarters like a great,
fat slug and Eva encourages her to be lazy and cheeky.'

'For your information, Pauline, I don't want Verity roam-
ing around the grounds, or you and Doreen for that matter.
In fact, none of you are allowed to go out unless you've got a
grown-up with you — and that's an order.'

Pauline blinked in disbelief. 'Why?'

'Good God, child, why do you think we have a guard
around the building? Because it's not safe, that's why, and,
from what I hear, you've been making friends with some
pretty unsavoury characters.'

A little rustle caught Pauline's attention. She turned and

saw her mother sitting on a high-backed chair in the corner by the window. Pauline gazed at her incredulously, wondering why she had not spoken before.

'Daddy means this Wolfgang boy, darling,' her mother said. 'We just can't have you going off into the forest with him.'

Pauline wanted to ask, 'What forest?' but she decided that attack would be the best form of defence. 'Eva says you're going to make him go away. You won't, will you, Mummy?'

Her mother laughed. 'Of course not, darling. But if you really want to be friends with him, he'll have to come here. There's masses of room for you both to play. Why don't you invite him to tea?'

The thought of Wolfgang sitting down to tea in the nursery made Pauline want to shout with laughter. She looked down at the floor while her lips twitched involuntarily into a smile.

'There,' her father said, obviously misunderstanding her expression. 'You see how easy it is to be good. And you're going to have to be good for a bit. Eva's going off on leave tomorrow and I don't want you being too much of a nuisance to your mother. Now, give us both a kiss and off you run.'

At the same time, in the nursery, Eva said to Verity, '*Liebchen*, if we had won the war; we, the Germans —' her voice trailed away. She was standing by the window, her face dreamy and remote as if she was looking at a scene of unbelievable beauty instead of the NAAFI hut.

Verity went up to her and tugged at her skirt. One of the more likeable things about Eva was that, far from minding her skirt being tugged, she seemed actively to like it. Now, she looked down at Verity, her florid face transformed by a radiant smile. Verity guessed she was dreaming of the past, so she asked gently, '*Bitte, was haben Sie gesagt, Eva?*' She spoke in German deliberately so that she would not break the spell.

Eva opened her arms and lifted Verity into her dream world. Verity looked down on the NAAFI hut and the rows of dark pines behind it. The little thaw that afternoon had melted some of the snow, but now it was freezing again. The trees and the hut were hung with icicles which shimmered with iridescent colours and, as Verity watched, the sun began to set, turning the little patches of snow which had stayed in the branches to a delicate pink.

She rested her feet surreptitiously on the radiator to ease some of her weight from Eva's arms. She did not want to be put down. She wanted to stay there with Eva and watch the afternoon die. Eva rested her cheek against Verity's head, then suddenly held her so fiercely that Verity began to struggle to get away. Eva lifted her down to the floor again and abruptly drew the curtains.

'What is it?' Verity asked.

Eva looked down with her normal face: a little rueful and a little resigned. She brushed Verity's cheek with the back of her hand. 'Ghosts, Fräulein mouse,' she said, 'only ghosts.'

She sat down in the wicker chair and took a torn stocking from the work-basket at her side. 'Turn the lamp for me, *Liebchen*.'

Verity climbed onto the footstool and reached up to turn the standard-lamp on, then she pulled the stool closer to the chair so she could sit at Eva's feet.

'I don't like ghosts,' she said.

Eva threaded a needle and began to darn the stocking. 'Not all ghosts are bad. Sometimes it is good to remember. Just now, just to think and to remember made me happy.'

'What do you like to remember best?' Verity asked, more to keep the conversation going than from any real interest.

Eva let her hands drop into her lap and sat back, smiling in the lamplight. 'Hitler,' she said simply.

Verity gasped with shock. 'You shouldn't like remembering him, Eva,' she said sternly. 'He was a very wicked man.'

Eva smiled and nodded. 'So you think because you did not know him, but to me he was my good, good friend.'

Verity stood up to emphasize her disapproval. 'He wasn't. He was very wicked and if you go on like that, you won't be my friend any more.'

'Ah, but tomorrow I go away, so it is easy for me to love my old friend, even if it makes my new friend angry.'

'What do you mean, you're going away?' Verity demanded. 'Where are you going?'

'I am going home.' She put an arm around Verity's shoulder and drew her close. 'Don't be angry, *Liebchen*. You cannot love for half your life and then just forget your friend. I did love the Führer. We all did. It is not wicked to love.'

Verity moved closer. 'I suppose not.'

Eva put down her darning and patted her lap, inviting Verity to climb up and have a cuddle. Verity accepted.

'You see?' Eva murmured. 'You would not like if I stopped loving you just because you lose a quarrel with your sister. That is the war, *Liebling*; just a silly quarrel and Hitler, he lost the quarrel, but that doesn't mean he is wicked, does it?'

Verity smiled and shook her head against Eva's shoulder. 'I'm glad you love me. I wish you weren't going away,' she whispered.

Eva kissed her and laughed softly. 'That you must not wish. I go to see my brother. I am very happy.'

'I didn't know you had a brother,' Verity murmured. 'Has your mother had a baby?'

Eva laughed again. 'Silly mouse. My mother, she is an old, old woman. She cannot have a baby. No, my brother, Kurt, is a brave soldier like the father. He has been in prison with the Russians. All this time I am thinking he is dead, but today I get a letter from Muttie: "great news! Kurt is alive and he is coming home!" ' She squeezed Verity closer. 'I am so happy.'

40

Verity snuggled against her. 'Did Kurt love Hitler?' she asked.

'Of course,' Eva said sharply. 'All good Germans love Hitler. Now go and play with the sisters. I have work to do.'

VII
Uncle Denis

'That's a bit more like it, old girl,' the Dreamer said as he sat himself down on Weener's bed. 'Two whole days of uninterrupted Mummy! Well, I've left my scallywags at home. Reckon you don't need me to bring you any dreams tonight.' Weener laughed aloud and Pauline sighed audibly.

'I'm glad you came anyway,' Weener said with the special voice of her brain. 'It's always good to see you and to have a natter.'

'Just how I feel myself.' The Dreamer lay back on her bed and smiled his fierce smile at the ceiling. 'I especially liked the bit about the hymns, didn't you?' Weener nodded enthusiastically. That Sunday afternoon had been the best afternoon of her life.

It had all started with their mother getting silly and very giggly. She told them that her name was not Mummy, but Lucy the cat, so every time anyone said anything to her, she answered with a 'meaow'. The game made Verity and Weener laugh until it hurt, but Pauline could not, or would not join in.

'I think this is all very silly,' she said at last.

'Meaow?'

Verity and Weener rolled on the settee, gasping and hugging each other.

'Stop it, Mummy!' Pauline's voice was stern and humourless. 'I mean, it *is* Sunday, you know. Don't you think you ought to be teaching us hymns, or something?'

For a few moments their mother laughed helplessly, but then she rallied and seemed to pull herself together. 'You're absolutely right, Pauline. Come on girls, help me push the

42

settee out of the way. I'm going to teach you all the hymns I know.'

They pushed the settee against the far wall and the two easy chairs flat on either side of the hearth. It made a big space of floor once the little tables had been stacked on the settee. Then, holding one another by the waist, they made a crocodile and started to march around the room with their mother singing, 'Onward Christian Soldiers' very clearly so that they could learn the words. Weener was just getting the hang of it when her mother started to act up again. 'Onward Christian soldiers, meaow, meaow,' she sang, instead of drawing the last word out to fit the tune. Fighting down the urge to giggle, Weener began to imitate her and Verity soon joined in. Pauline was left singing the hymn properly as loudly as she could in the hope of drowning her family's irreverence.

They had just got to 'like a mighty army, meaow, meaow' when the doorbell rang and their mother stopped singing instantly and looked a little sheepish. 'Oh dear,' she said conspiratorially, 'I hope that's not somebody come to complain.'

They all stood still while she went to answer the door. 'I say,' it was a man's voice and it sounded very disgruntled. 'I mean, it *is* Sunday, you know.'

'I *am* sorry,' their mother's voice was softly apologetic. 'I was just teaching my little girls some hymns. They'll be going to Sunday school soon, you see.'

'Good heavens, was that was it was? Thought you'd got the "Sally Ally" in there. Can I come in? Know some pretty good hymns myself.'

There was a slight bustle and then he was with them. 'I'm the rude old buzzard from downstairs,' he told them. 'Come on girls, let's get marching.' He took his place at the head of the crocodile and Pauline's voice was soon swamped with a chorus of meaows.

But, as if that were not enough, their father turned up in the middle of it all with a man called Uncle Denis.

'Are you a real uncle?' Verity asked suspiciously.

' 'Course I am. I'm Uncle Denis who's a menace.' He swung her into the air and settled her on his shoulders. 'Watch out all of you.' He eyed them all with a terrifying look. 'We're a witch and we're coming to get you!'

Weener squealed and hung onto her father's legs. 'Daddy, Daddy!' she shrieked in mock terror and amazingly, he swung her on to his shoulders and whooped after Uncle Denis and Verity. Weener was so high in the air that her head was brushing the ceiling. Her father had never lifted her up before and she was so excited that she kept bouncing up and down on his shoulders and shouting, 'We're the biggest witch! We are, aren't we, Daddy?'

' 'Course we are, my poppet,' he shouted as he charged straight at Uncle Denis, then dodged past him so close that Verity's hair tickled right across her face.

Suddenly, Pauline was on the man from downstairs' shoulders and all three men were careering around the room; charging, feinting, wheeling, with the girls screaming on their shoulders.

Uncle Denis did a little dance so that Verity's face bobbed up and down in front of Weener. 'Tee hee hee! Tee hee hee!' he sang. 'Can't catch us for a toffee flea!' then he charged out of the room. The man from downstairs rushed after him and soon Weener found herself flying along in hot pursuit. She dug her fingers into her father's hair. It was thick and curly, like Verity's.

'Ow!' he shouted. 'My witch keeps pulling my hair.'

'Serve you right, you silly old witch,' Uncle Denis sang as he burst through the nursery door. Verity, who only ducked just in time, screamed. 'Put me down. Put me down,' she begged. 'I'm getting frightened.' Weener crouched low on her father's shoulders and felt the door-frame brush her shoulders.

Uncle Denis was bounding around the room like a mountain goat; jumping over the footstool and climbing over the chairs, while Verity flopped limply on his shoulders. The man from downstairs and her father were much taller than he was, so they did not try to follow him. 'Cowardy, cowardy custards,' he sang at them, 'we're the best witch in the world.' Then he wheeled suddenly and tore back to the drawing-room.

'Please,' Verity pleaded. 'Please, I want to get down.'

Weener whispered in her father's ear, 'I think she's getting frightened, Daddy.' He patted her legs as the man from downstairs ran past with Pauline.

'He won't drop her, poppet,' he said and, to Weener's immense relief, he walked quietly down the hall.

'What now?' asked the man from downstairs, once they were all in the drawing-room again.

'Ring a ring a roses,' Uncle Denis said decisively, and the three men joined hands and danced round and round, singing the words in funny voices. The girls hung on and kept their balance until the men got to 'atishoo atishoo. We all fall down,' when they all flopped to the floor and let the girls roll off their shoulders.

Uncle Denis closed his eyes and lay on his back for a few moments. Weener went over and looked at him closely, just in case he was dead. He did not move so she knelt down and pulled up his eyelid. 'Are you dead?' she asked.

One bright, black eye glittered wickedly at her. 'Not likely, my lovely,' he said. 'But I couldn't half use a drink.' That statement seemed to bring everybody to their senses. They pulled the furniture back into place and started to behave like grown-ups again.

Weener always found grown-ups very boring when they started to drink, so she wandered over to the window and looked out. A big, black car had pulled up in the drive and a man in black jodhpurs and high, black leather boots was stamping up and down in the snow beside it.

'Do you know,' she said to no one in particular, 'there's a huge black car down there.'

'Damn,' Uncle Denis said in a conversational tone. 'Bloody Hun, I told him to give me a couple of hours.'

'Another drink?' her father asked.

The phone rang and Uncle Denis stood up. 'That'll be the service staff to say the car's arrived. Shall I get it?' Without waiting for anyone to reply, he picked up the receiver. 'Yep.' he barked into the mouthpiece, 'Tell him to wait.' Then he slammed the phone down again. 'Bloody Krauts,' he muttered, and took a swig from his glass. He rolled the liquid around his mouth thoughtfully, then swallowed it and rubbed his hands together. 'Right, you girls,' he said briskly, 'time for your drawing lesson. Come on, gather round. No loitering there.'

He sat down on the settee and pulled a notepad out of his pocket and unscrewed the top of his pen. Weener and her sisters crowded round while he drew an oblong shape with a domed top.

'Right, now what's that?' he asked sternly.

They looked at it from all angles in silence.

'Dear, dear,' Uncle Denis's voice was reproving. 'You're not so clever as I thought you were. Doesn't the fact that I've drawn it in red ink mean anything to you?'

They shook their heads.

'Oh well, I'll just have to finish it off then.' A few quick strokes turned it into the back view of a pink elephant.

'Draw us another one, please, Uncle Denis,' Weener begged.

'I'll need another drink first. Here,' he handed her his empty glass. Feeling very important, Weener took it in both her hands and carefully carried it over to the drinks trolley. The grown-ups laughed and her father came up and put his hand on her shoulder.

'Better let me help you, poppet. I don't want you slipping him a mickey finn.'

Weener smiled up at him and suddenly she was glad that they had come all this way to be with him. He poured the drink and she carried it carefully back to the settee.

While she had been away, Uncle Denis had drawn three

pink elephants in graded size and labelled them Pauline, Doreen and Verity Elephant.

'Draw a daddy elephant,' Weener said.

Uncle Denis looked at the paper critically. 'H'm. We'll have to have a clean sheet for that. By my reckoning, daddy elephants come pretty large.'

There was an apologetic tap on the door. Uncle Denis half twisted to look over the back of the settee. One of the waiters from downstairs stood in the doorway.

'Please sir, the chauffeur, he ask me to say the car is here.'

Uncle Denis turned back to his drawing. 'I know.' he said simply. There was a tense silence for some moments and then the waiter coughed politely. 'What would you like for me to tell him, please?' Uncle Denis finished his elephant and then drew the tail with meticulous care. 'I've already told him to wait.' he said quietly.

'But he ask me to say —'

'I have told him to wait.' There was a terrifying steely edge to his voice that made Weener nearly wet her knickers. She bit her lip and looked up at the waiter. He was very pale, but there was a determined set to his face.

'I —' he began, but Uncle Denis suddenly whipped round. His face was flushed and his eyes glittered with hatred.

'*Raus!*' he shouted, and the waiter melted into the shadows of the hall. 'And close the bloody door!' Uncle Denis added savagely. The door swung noiselessly to. Only the slight click of the catch showed that there was anybody behind it. Uncle Denis swallowed down the rest of his drink.

'Bloody Kraut.' he muttered. 'How the hell did he get in here?'

'The service entrance.' her mother said quietly. Weener looked at her gratefully. Somehow her voice had broken the tension.

Uncle Denis's glass was refilled and he drew a whole army of elephants. Then he drew elephants standing on a washing-line; elephants in the bath; elephants in the sky, parachuting down with open umbrellas in their trunks. From the

47

one simple design, he could make an endless variety, and each new drawing took them by surprise, making them gasp and giggle while the glass kept emptying and being refilled.

The light began to fade and her mother smiled across at her. 'Turn the lamp on, will you, darling?'

After Weener had turned on the light, she could not resist going over to the window to see what the chauffeur was doing. He must have noticed the light go on in the window because he put his hand through the car window and started honking his horn.

Verity stood up and followed Weener over to the window. 'He's getting ever so cross, Uncle Denis.' she said. Weener kicked Verity's ankle and hissed, 'Shut up.' down her ear. Verity gasped with indignation. 'Shut up' was one of the expressions they were never allowed to use. 'Well he is,' she said angrily. 'He's getting crosser and crosser. He's so cross he's stamping. You'll have to go, Uncle Denis. He'll never forgive you, you know.'

Uncle Denis laughed a short, hard laugh. 'I'll teach him to be cross. I'll have the bloody Hun beaten within an inch of his life if I get any more nonsense from him.'

Verity's face drooped. 'Don't! You mustn't. He's only cross because he's cold.'

Their mother stood up. 'Good heavens,' she said. 'Is that the time? You must all be starving. Come along, darlings, it's time for your tea.'

'Is Uncle Denis having tea with us?' Verity asked.

'No, of course he isn't. Now give him a nice big kiss, all of you.'

'And don't forget the rude old buzzard from downstairs.'

They all looked at him in surprise. He had been so quiet, sitting in the corner, that they had forgotten all about him. Weener went over and kissed him. 'Shall we see you again?' she asked against his scratchy cheek.

' 'Fraid not, darling. I'm off tomorrow. Perhaps we'll meet up sometime.' He gave her a little hug and Weener found herself liking him much more than Uncle Denis.

'I hope we do,' she said.

Uncle Denis's cheek was very smooth, but she felt no warmth from him when she kissed him. 'You mustn't mind Verity,' she told him. 'She's only soppy because she's so young.'

He smacked her bottom playfully. 'You rotten little tike. I think she's a smashing girl.'

'Well, she's all right,' Weener tried to explain, but her mother called her away so she was not able to tell him how Verity always managed to spoil things so that everybody ended up either in bed or in the nursery.

'Still,' the Dreamer interrupted Weener's thoughts, 'you do quite like Verity, you know, old girl.'

Weener blinked. 'Gosh, have I been asleep, Dreamer?' she asked.

'For heaven's sake!' Pauline shouted through the darkness. 'Stop that damn muttering, Weener.'

Verity turned in her sleep and started to snore.

'Now look what you've done,' Pauline said desperately. 'You've started Verity off. Honestly, between the two of you, I never get a wink of sleep.'

'See what I mean?' the Dreamer said. 'She's a lot less nuisance than that Pauline.'

'Shut up!' Pauline shouted, and the Dreamer laughed softly as he snuggled down beside Weener.

'Bet she's wetted her bed again,' he whispered. 'Thank heavens *she*'s not my dream child.'

VIII
Kurt

To Weener's surprise, the Dreamer was still beside her when she woke the next morning.

'Thought I'd stick around, old girl,' he explained, 'because I had a smashing idea while you were asleep.'

Weener hugged herself with excitement. 'What?'

'Well, Pauline's hair is black and Verity's is yellow, but yours is a bit ordinary, if you don't mind me saying so.'

Weener nodded her agreement.

'Well, if you got a comb, stuck it in the end and wound it round and round, it would look like a sausage roll on the top of your head. That would be a bit different, wouldn't it?'

Something hit Weener on the ear. She opened her eyes and saw it was one of the hard little pillows that none of them could get used to. Pauline was sitting up in bed, looking furious. 'You damn well muttered all through the damn night. I'm damn well not having you muttering all through the morning too.' Weener shrugged and closed her eyes again, but the Dreamer had gone.

'Are you asleep, Weener, or were you talking to your Dreamer?' Verity asked.

Weener humped herself under the bedclothes. 'Mind your own damn business.' she muttered.

'Vety,' Pauline's voice was soft and coaxing, 'Weener's got my pillow. If you let me share yours, you can come and have a cuddle.'

Weener heard Verity thump out of bed and pad across the floor. Twerp, she thought; honestly, she's so stupid, she always falls for it.

'Your bed doesn't half smell, Pauline,' she heard Verity say.

'That's because I've just let off a pooh. Don't worry, it'll soon go off.'

Weener heard Verity climb into Pauline's bed and then a lot of rustling as she tried to get comfortable.

'It's all wet.' she said indignantly.

Of course it's wet, Weener thought; why do you think she asked you in for a cuddle, you twerp. She tried to drift back to sleep, but she was too irritated to relax. The day had begun and, as usual, it had begun badly. She rolled over onto her back and opened her eyes.

The light was quite strong behind the curtains, which meant it must be nearly breakfast time. There did not seem to be much point in lying there now that the Dreamer had gone, so she rolled out of bed and padded across to the window.

'Hey!' Verity said indignantly as Weener drew the curtains, but Weener ignored her. She wandered over to the little white painted chest of drawers that served them all as a dressing table and peered into the triple mirror.

The Dreamer had been absolutely right about her hair, she decided. It was halfway between yellow and brown; real Weener hair, she told herself. She started to undo her night plaits and sighed because she looked such a very ordinary little girl. She saw what the Dreamer meant about the sausage roll. It would make her face look pointed and witchy: she might even look a bit exciting.

She combed her hair to one side, put the comb in the end and began to roll it into her hair. She had not realized how many times she would need to roll it round and soon her arms began to ache with the effort of being held high. She gave them a bit of a rest and then started again. The problem now was that she could not remember which direction she had been rolling in. She gave the comb a few twists, then realized, too late, that she had been winding in the wrong direction. The strange thing was that, instead of the sausage

51

roll coming undone, her hair seemed to be getting into a horrible muddle. She quickly twisted back towards the crown of her head. The hair at the side of her scalp tweaked and pulled with each turn of the comb.

Weener began to panic. The comb was now deeply embedded in her hair and whichever way she twisted it, her hair only became more inextricably tangled. The most disappointing thing about it all was that it looked nothing like a sausage roll.

'What are you doing, Weener?' Verity's reflection bobbed at the bottom of the mirror.

'I've got the comb stuck. I can't get it out.'

Verity climbed onto a little chair which stood beside the chest of drawers. 'I'll get it out for you. Come closer so I can reach.' Weener dropped her arms gratefully and moved closer. 'Gosh, thanks, Vety. My arms don't half ache.'

Verity did not reply because she was concentrating on untangling the comb. Weener could not see what she was doing, but it hurt dreadfully. Verity gave a sudden tug which made Weener shout with pain and pull back involuntarily. The little chair toppled and Verity crashed to the floor.

'What on earth is going on?' Their mother stood in the doorway. Pauline got out of bed and walked over to her.

'I'm afraid Verity's wetted my bed, Mummy. I had her in for a cuddle, you see. Still, we mustn't blame her, really. I mean she is still very young.'

Her mother bent down, her eyes twinkling with amusement. She cupped her hand momentarily around Pauline's bottom. 'Then would you mind telling me how your pyjamas came to be wet?'

Pauline felt the trousers for herself. 'Damn,' she muttered, 'they must have mopped the wee-wee up, I suppose.'

For a moment, Weener thought her mother was going to laugh, but instead, the little muscles around her mouth tightened. 'Don't use that word Pauline. Swearing is a very nasty habit. Off you go to the lavatory and then you can strip the bed down.'

Weener admired her mother for that. If it had been Eva, Pauline would probably have taken her in. She looked down at Verity who was still sitting on the floor with her mouth open. 'Stand up.' she whispered urgently.

In response, Verity began to sob loudly. Weener knew she was not really crying because she had her knuckles pressed against her eyes. But, though her mother could always see through Pauline's tricks, Verity could invariably fool her. Now, she bent down and lifted Verity into her arms.

'Darling, darling,' she murmured, 'what is it?'

'I fell off the chair,' Verity sobbed.

Her mother carried her over to Weener's bed and sat down with her on her knee. 'Now shhh,' she soothed. 'How did you fall off? Where does it hurt?'

Verity only sobbed.

Weener came over to where they were sitting. 'It's all right, Mummy,' she said. 'She's not really crying.'

Her mother looked up and her expression quickly turned to shock. 'Weener,' she gasped, 'what have you done to your hair?' Verity looked up from the sanctuary of her mother's arms and bit her lip. Weener felt herself colour. 'I got the comb stuck, Mummy.' she said lamely.

Her mother patted the bed. 'Come on, we'll have to try and get it out for you.'

Weener sat down while her mother reached around Verity and tried to untangle the knotted comb.

'You must have been twiddling it in your hair,' she said at last. 'Weener, why did you do it?'

'My Dreamer told me to. He said it would look like a sausage roll on the top of my head. Ouch!' she added involuntarily. Her mother let go of the comb and lifted Verity to the ground.

'Go and get washed, darling,' she said.

'I can't. Pauline's in the bathroom.'

'Well, go and tell her to hurry up.'

Verity padded off obediently and, once they were alone, her mother took Weener by the shoulders. 'Now, look

53

darling, you must stop all this nonsense about your Dreamer. He's only in your imagination. He isn't alive and he doesn't tell you to do these silly things.'

Weener looked down at the floor. 'He does.' she muttered mutinously.

Her mother put her hand under her chin and tilted it so that Weener had to look at her. 'He doesn't, Doreen. And, you know, you're getting much too big to play these silly games. Now, I'm going to have to cut this comb out of your hair and Daddy, who *is* real, is going to be very unhappy when he sees you without your plaits.' Weener stared back at her blankly. The Dreamer was one of the few points on which she knew they would never agree.

'Where does Eva keep her scissors?' her mother asked.

'In the work-box in the nursery.' Weener replied.

While her mother went to fetch them, Weener closed her eyes and willed the Dreamer to appear. If only he would appear just once when her mother was there, she would have to admit that he did exist and that Weener was not a liar. But he either could not, or would not hear her and, when her mother came back with the scissors, Weener gave up and resigned herself to being misunderstood.

She felt the scissors go into her hair, just under the comb. 'Keep very still,' her mother told her.

Weener bit her lip and tried to obey, but a sudden scream from the bathroom made her jump just as her mother was cutting. The scissors slipped and chopped the hair too close to her scalp. The comb flopped down by her ear, suspended by the last bit of the tangle.

'Oh, my God!' her mother breathed.

Suddenly Verity was with them. She was really crying this time and cradling her left ear with both her hands. 'Pauline hit me,' she sobbed. 'I told her you said she'd got to hurry up and she hit me.'

Pauline came stomping through from the nursery. 'I didn't.' she shouted angrily. She made a grab at Verity's arm and Verity let out an earsplitting scream.

'Stop it!' their mother shouted above the noise. 'Both of you stop it immediately!'

Pauline's face was red and furious. 'I won't!' she shouted back. 'She's a damn liar and I won't have her damn well cheeking me the way she does.'

'Don't you dare use that language to me, Pauline. Verity, let me see your ear.'

Verity took her hands away for a moment, revealing a huge, mauve ear. She started to jump up and down while real tears ran down her cheeks. 'Oh,' she gasped as she covered it up again, 'it doesn't half hurt.'

'Pauline, how dare you do that to your sister!'

'I didn't. She hit it on the wall. She's a liar.'

'I'm not!' Verity bellowed.

'Yes you are. You're a liar and a sneak!'

Suddenly their mother moved. She caught Pauline by the arm, took off her slipper and slapped her several times across the bottom with it. 'Now,' she commanded, 'go into the nursery. Stand in the corner and don't you dare move until I say you may.' She lifted Verity up. 'Go on,' she said threateningly to Pauline, 'I won't tell you twice.'

Pauline wavered, then meekly obeyed.

'Come on, poppet,' her mother said as she carried Verity through to the bathroom. 'We'll bathe that ear for you.'

Weener hated it when Pauline and Verity quarrelled. It gave her a sickening, dragging feeling in her stomach. She felt flat and a bit frightened sitting there alone on her bed. She put a tentative hand to her head to feel for the comb.

'Miss Doreen! What have you done to your beautiful hair?' It was Eva's voice, but Weener could not really believe she was there. She turned and saw Eva standing beside the open service door.

'Eva!' she gasped with relief. She stood up and ran to her. 'Oh Eva,' she breathed as she threw her arms around her, 'it's smashing to have you back again.'

Eva bent down and held her close. 'I did not think you liked me,' she said with surprise.

55

Weener kissed her cheek. 'Oh, I do. I love you. Did you have a nice time?'

Eva barked out a harsh little laugh, then straightened up and taking Weener by the hand, led her over to her bed. 'As you have begun to cut, we must go on. Perhaps it will not look so bad.'

'How was Kurt?' Weener asked as Eva started to clip her hair. Eva worked in silence for some minutes, then sat back and eyed Weener with cold appraisal. 'A little more from the side.' she said abstractedly.

'But how was he, Eva? Had he grown since you saw him last?' Eva's face softened momentarily, but she quickly pulled it back into a mask of firmness.

'He was dead, *Liebchen*. They only let him go because he was dying. He died on the train and when we went to meet, he was grey and cold; just sitting there on the wooden seat. So many were dead, they did not even close his eyes.'

Weener felt a pang of horror. Something about the simplicity of Eva's statement made her see the train and Kurt sitting dead and cold with all the other grey, sightless men. She took Eva's hand and held it gently. 'Poor Eva.' she whispered.

Eva rested her cheek on Weener's cropped head. 'Poor Germany, you should be saying. All those brave men who went to fight: so proud, so beautiful. And now they are grey, broken and dead. Who will fight for Germany when so many are dead?'

Weener squeezed her hand. 'I will Eva,' she said warmly. 'I'll fight for you, honestly I will.' She felt a warm tear ooze onto her scalp.

'No *Liebchen*, you must fight for other things. And I: I must work. It is the only way I can forget, if I work.'

They sat for some moments in silence and then Eva asked suddenly, 'Where are the sisters?'

'Pauline hit Verity, so she's standing in the corner and Mummy's in the bathroom, bathing Verity's ear.'

Eva laughed briefly and bitterly. 'So,' she said, pulling the corners of her mouth down, 'so, I think the mother will be glad I have come home.'

IX
The house in the forest

It was nearly two weeks since Eva had returned and now the Spring was really beginning to come. In clumps, beneath the trees, the first snowdrops had begun to appear. They were veined in delicate green, which was accentuated by the darker, braver green of their resilient leaves. By day, the thawing wind shook their bell-like flowers so that they seemed to be dancing in the snow, while the droplets of melted ice sparkled and fell amongst them. At night, the bitter frosts froze all things into silence, so that each new morning saw the grounds of the Kaiserhof transformed into a sugar landscape of icicles and pastel lightness.

Verity had discovered that they really were in a forest: a beautiful forest that grew darker and more mysterious on each exploration.

Pauline and Weener were very busy in the playroom, building an aeroplane out of Meccano. Pauline was pretty sure that when it was finished, it would actually fly. They would not let Verity help them because she was too young and might well spoil it. For the first few days, she sat on the rocking-horse and watched them, but it was very disheartening to watch anything so exciting and not be allowed to join in.

Eventually, Eva suggested that she and Verity should start taking Goldie for walks. Eva thought it might even stop him from being so fat. To begin with, he was not at all keen on the idea and after only a few hundred yards, he would sit down in the snow and beg with his eyes for Verity to take him home. The sight of his beseeching, helpless face made her long to carry him or to let him go back to his favourite place beneath the radiator in the nursery. But Eva told her she must be firm with him. She said that dogs would never love a person who was soft. Verity knew this was true because, although he was politely affectionate with her, it was Pauline whom he really adored and Pauline was horribly hard with him.

So each day, she and Eva walked Goldie just a little bit further. At first Verity did it to make him love her as much as Pauline, but as the days went by, she began to love walking in the forest and to long to explore deeper and deeper into that overpowering, half-lit world. Goldie began to love it too. He walked more easily now and sometimes he would even chase off on his own, his ridiculous ears flapping and his great, feathery feet churning up the snow.

They found Wolfgang's hut, but he was not there. Nobody had seen anything of him since that day Pauline told Weener about their friendship. Verity supposed that, like the wild dogs, he sometimes went into the forest to hunt for food.

They found a little house that Eva said had once been used by German officers when they went hunting. Verity was enchanted with it, but they could not explore because it was all locked up. 'One day, when the mother is in a good mood,' Eva promised, 'I shall speak to her and ask if I can bring you here to sleep.' Verity hugged herself with anticipation. She was sure that her mother must be getting into a very good mood because Eva had been giving her all sorts of lovely things lately.

Now, when the nursery meals came up from the kitchen, the girls had to be very quick if they wanted to get enough to eat. Any little cakes, bread rolls or even slices of meat that stayed a second too long on the plate were snatched up by Eva. 'Ah,' she would say, 'so you are not wanting this. I shall save for the mother.' She would not let them have the milk and sugar that was sent up for their tea either. When they protested, she made them feel really ashamed of themselves. 'The mother is an old woman,' she told them sternly.

'Would you want that she should go without milk and sugar for her tea just so that you shall have it?'

They all shook their heads and, though none of them liked tea without milk and sugar, they began to get used to it.

Verity was sure that her mother would soon be in such a good mood that she would not be able to refuse to let Eva take her to stay in the little house in the forest. She was beginning to forget what her mother had been like in England: in fact, she sometimes went for days on end without remembering England at all. On those days, it felt as if she had always been in the Kaiserhof with Eva and Goldie, but though she had every reason to be happy, a feeling always nagged at the back of her mind, telling her that it was not so and that something, somewhere, was terribly wrong.

Though Goldie did not get any thinner, he became much more alert and he lost his air of only wanting to be left alone. Verity and Eva began to teach him tricks. Now, if anybody threw a stick for him, he would chase through the snow to fetch it and if Verity shouted, 'Die,' he would roll over on his back with his legs straight up in the air.

'Is he very old?' Verity asked one day.

'No, *Liebling*, it was only because the man who had him before you was very lazy. He never took him walking like we do so he got fat and stupid. If he had been turned out to run wild, he would have died.'

Verity looked at Goldie who was digging feverishly in the soft snow. 'Thank goodness we came here, then. He *is* getting stronger and very much more clever, isn't he?'

Eva patted her cheek. 'Of course he is, but even if he wasn't, he won't be turned out now because he's got you.'

Verity nodded enthusiastically. 'Let's take him down to the river today. He loves it down there.' She kept her eyes very steady while she spoke so that Eva would not know she was lying. Her real reason for wanting to go that way was because it took them past the little house, and she hoped it might remind Eva of her promise.

They followed the path which had been cut through the

60

even rows of tall, dark pine trees. Verity lingered for a moment, gazing up to the very top of the forest: stretching her imagination to the tip of the highest tree. She liked to do this because, when she brought her mind back to earth again, it showed how small and unimportant she and Eva were. It eased her ache of unhappiness to realize her insignificance. Somehow it seemed to minimise her sadness.

'What are you doing?' Eva barked from a little way along the path. 'You will stay with me, please.'

Verity ran to her, feeling spider-like and tiny. 'Oh Eva,' she gasped, 'imagine being as tall as the trees.'

Eva snorted. 'What nonsense. Then you would fall down on your face.'

Verity felt her eyes twinkling, but she kept a deadpan face. 'Was Hitler as tall as the trees?' she asked innocently.

'You will not mock the Führer.' Eva turned on her heel. 'Already I have told you that one who was as tall as the trees would fall down on his face.'

Verity took her hand and squeezed it to show she was sorry. Eva had been so sad and so touchy since she came home. Often she thought the girls were being rude or unkind when actually, they were only joking. More often still, she would weep. Sitting over the sewing-basket or tidying the nursery, quite suddenly tears would flood from her eyes, although she never sobbed and never spoke of her sorrow. She had a cloak of sadness around her which made Verity feel strangely protective.

'I'm sorry. I was only being silly,' she said now. 'Come on, let's go and look at the little house.'

Hand in hand they walked on down the path, round its well organized turn and up to the back of the shooting-lodge. Here, Verity broke away and ran to peep in through the windows. 'Eva,' she shouted, 'Eva, come quickly. Someone's been here and changed all the furniture around.'

She ran around the side of the house and then stopped dead. The smooth white sweep of snow that led down to the river was churned up with yellow, muddy tyre tracks. The river path was spoilt too and the little house was no longer private and enchanting, but loud with the feeling of violation.

'Who?' she asked as Eva joined her by the front verandah, 'who could have done it, Eva?'

Eva laughed. 'It was the mother, silly goose. On Saturday she was giving a dinner party here. And that makes me think,' she put a note of excitement into her voice, 'this morning, I speak to the mother. I have a good surprise for you.'

'What?' Verity asked eagerly, although she had really guessed.

'Ah, it is a surprise, so we must wait till tea-time when I can tell the sisters too.'

All the way back to the Kaiserhof, Verity hugged herself with excitement. They would have to put all the furniture back in its right place, of course, and clear up the mess the jeeps had made of the snow, but it would not take long and then everything would be perfect.

She sat through nursery tea in an agony of fear in case Pauline should be naughty and the trip called off. There was a swiss roll for sweet with a big jug of custard to go over it. Eva had the knife poised, ready to cut it into slices.

'Only a small piece for me, thank you, Eva,' Verity said ingratiatingly, 'and no custard, thank you. We must remember the mother is old. I should not want to eat swiss roll and custard while the mother had none.'

Pauline and Weener shot her a look of undisguised loathing. Verity smiled back at them sweetly. 'How's your aeroplane, Pauline?' she asked.

'Mind your own damn business, crawler.' Pauline muttered. 'I'll have a nice big piece, please Eva; seeing as Verity has looked after the mother's share.'

Eva's face darkened. The knife hovered as if undecided on how small a piece it could get away with. In the end Eva and the knife compromised with a medium sized slice.

'Hey!' Pauline's indignation was automatic. 'What a mingy, rotten, little bit!'

'Ha! You complain! You, who have everything; you complain! Do you know there are people starving in Germany?'

Pauline and Eva glared at one another across the table as the tension mounted and then Weener said quietly, 'Actually, it's finished.'

Everybody turned to her in surprise. 'What is?' Verity asked for them all.

'The aeroplane,' Weener said laconically. 'And it didn't fly. I think Meccano's rotten stuff.' She pushed her chair back and gazed with boredom at the swiss roll. 'I've finished —' she started to say, but Verity kicked her ankle and gave her a look that warned her against leaving the table. 'Playing with Meccano.' she improvised a little lamely.

'Eva,' Verity was careful to keep the note of excitement out of her voice, 'didn't you say you had a surprise for us?' Eva looked at them all narrowly, as if she were not sure whether they could be trusted with anything as important as a surprise. 'Oh please, Eva,' Verity threw caution to the wind. 'We've been ever so good and you promised to tell us at tea-time.'

Eva's face relaxed. 'All right, *Liebling*, for you I will tell. On Saturday, I am taking you all for a little holiday.'

Verity looked hard at the tablecloth and then slid an excited smile at Weener. 'Where are we going, Eva?' she asked innocently.

'We go to stay with my mother. I think you will like very much.' Verity looked up at her. Her astonishment was so great that, at this moment, there was no room for disappointment.

'Is your mother German?' Weener asked.

'Of course she is. Why do you ask me such a stupid question?'

Weener shrugged. 'I just wondered where she lived, because, to be quite candid, I don't want to go anywhere except back to England.' Verity expected an explosion of anger, but instead, Eva stood up and went over to Weener.

'I know you long for your home, *Liebchen*,' she said with awkward compassion. 'But it will get better with the Spring and you will like it with my mother, you will see.'

As Verity watched them, the shock subsided and now she felt sick with disappointment. She was afraid she might start crying at the table, so she pushed her chair back and said, 'I've finished my tea. May I leave the table, please?'

Eva nodded and Verity went over to where Goldie was drowsing under the radiator. She lay down beside him and lifted one of his long, curly ears. 'I thought we were going to take you to the little house,' she whispered. 'I'm sorry you've got to make do with Eva's rotten mother.'

He lifted his head and licked her face to show he did not really mind. Verity kissed him, then, to show him how deeply he was loved, she began to lick his muzzle and round behind his ears.

'Yeuk!' Pauline said disdainfully from the table. 'Verity's licking Goldie's ears. Honestly, she *is* revolting.'

Eva swooped down on Verity. 'Never,' she said sternly as she lifted her abruptly from the floor, 'never, never let me see you do that again.'

'Anyway, it's my dog.' Pauline casually cut a lump from the swiss roll and held it out. 'Here, Goldie,' she called encouragingly.

With Verity under one arm, Eva rushed at Pauline and slapped her wrist. 'You do not give good food to the dog!'

'Right ho.' Pauline's voice took on a spiteful, nasal twang. She popped the lump of swiss roll into her mouth while she glared defiantly at Eva. 'I'll eat it, then,' she added. Goldie rolled his eyes and his face drooped with disappointment.

'Oh, poor Goldie!' Verity shouted as she struggled against Eva's grip. 'You've got to give him some. You promised him.' Eva slapped Pauline's legs, then set Verity down and slapped her too. 'What was that for?' Verity asked as the tears welled in her eyes.

'For licking the dog's ears and encouraging your sister. You will all go to bed now, please. You have been so wicked, I shall have to see whether I can still take you to my mother.'

As they got ready for bed, Weener whispered, 'I don't care if she doesn't take us to her rotten mother. It would only be horrible like every other rotten day in this rotten place.'

'You will not talk, please.' Eva shouted from the nursery. Verity sighed. Weener, as usual, was probably right.

X
Frau Königsberg

Frau Königsberg turned out to be completely terrifying. She was the epitome of Weener's worst nightmares of a witch. Shaped like a water-butt, she was swathed in an indeterminate number of jerseys and cardigans and her skirt was as shapeless and greenish black as were her wrinkled woollen stockings. She wore checked, felt carpet slippers, one of which had lost its pompom. Weener could have learned to live with all this, if only God had given the woman a nice face. But Frau Königsberg's face was the worst thing about her. It was a sunken, shrivelled prune, dominated by hard, observant eyes that glittered unnaturally black against the pallid skin. A thousand little lines were etched around the curiously caved-in mouth, with a deep black line at each corner, stretching down to the chin.

'Crumbs!' Weener breathed as Frau Königsberg appeared in her doorway to welcome them. She turned to look at their driver who was just climbing back into the jeep. 'Isn't he staying with us, Eva?' she asked, with a sinking feeling of alarm.

'Of course not, *Liebchen*. He will return on Monday to take you home.'

Weener heard the engine start up and watched the jeep drive away. She waved, but the driver did not wave back and, once he had gone, a total silence settled on the flat, empty landscape.

Eva patted her encouragingly on the shoulder. 'You did not expect that my mother lived in the country, I think?'

Weener turned back to Frau Königsberg. The expression

had not changed. 'Why is her mouth such a funny shape?' she whispered.

'Don't be rude!' Eva whispered back. She turned to Frau Königsberg. 'Darling Mummy,' she said in German, 'here are Miss Pauline, Miss Doreen and my darling, little Miss Verity.'

Frau Königsberg hissed at them to come in and, as she smiled, Weener noticed that her gums were completely bereft of teeth. She looked up at Eva. 'She hasn't got any teeth.' she whispered.

Inside, the cottage was like a cave: a dark and secret cavern where all that was evil might hide. Weener felt isolated and very frightened.

'Why hasn't she got any teeth?' she demanded and then gasped at the level of her own voice.

Frau Königsberg beckoned her forward and, against her will, Weener found herself complying. Frau Königsberg caught her wrist and pulled her hand towards the sunken, gaping mouth. Half fascinated, half repelled, Weener allowed her hand to be directed on a tour of inspection of Frau Königsberg's bald gums. There was not a tooth left in her head, but as Weener came to the last bit of the lower back jaw, the gums suddenly snapped to and caught her finger in a vice-like grip. Weener shouted aloud in surprise and pain.

Frau Königsberg gazed down on her for a few seconds and then let go. '*Und* now you know how it is that I eat.' she observed drily. They were the only English words she spoke throughout the whole weekend.

Outside, playing in the boring back-yard, Verity asked, 'Why did you let her do it, Weener?'

Weener thought for a moment and then shuddered. 'I don't know,' she said, 'but it was absolutely horrible.'

'I think there's something pretty fishy about that woman,' Pauline told them seriously. 'Come on,' she started forward, nodding her head towards the gateway, 'let's go somewhere she can't hear us. We're going to have a conference about all this.'

Weener and Verity followed her out to the flat, deserted road that ran in front of the cottage. Weener could not help feeling excited. It was the first time for ages that Pauline had included both her and Verity in her games.

She closed the gate carefully behind her as if, in some way, that would stop Frau Königsberg from overhearing them. 'Do you think she's a witch, then Pauline?' she whispered.

Pauline snorted with contempt. 'Of course not!' she said in a normal voice. 'There's no such thing as witches.'

'What then?' Verity asked timidly.

'If you ask me, she's up to her neck in something — something really fishy,' Pauline answered.

Weener gasped. 'What, like murdering people?' she asked.

Pauline nodded. 'Something like that. What we've got to ask ourselves now is, "what are *we* going to do about it?" '

'Gosh,' Weener breathed.

They trailed along the road for some minutes in silence and then Verity asked, 'What *are* we going to do about it, Pauline?'

'I'm glad you asked that, Verity.' Pauline stopped walking suddenly and faced them both. 'I think we should form a secret society. We'll call it "The Society for Looking Into and Investigating Things that are Strange". We will, of course, be putting ourselves in appalling danger and it's no good either of you joining if you're going to be babyish about it. You've got to be completely fearless and swear you'll never give away the secrets of the society.'

'Wow!' All at once, Weener felt brave, mysterious and very important. 'I swear, Pauline. Honestly I do.'

Pauline nodded. 'Good,' she said briskly. 'I'll be the captain and Weener, here, can be the vice-captain.'

'What about me?' Verity asked sulkily. 'Why can't I be something? I'm never allowed to be anything. It isn't fair.'

Pauline eyed her coldly. 'Are you surprised, when you

behave like that? I had been going to say that you could be the chief investigator, but, when you go all sulky and babyish, it makes me wonder whether I can even let you be a member.'

Verity's face drooped for a moment, but then, from somewhere, she seemed to find a new resolve. 'I promise I'll never be babyish again,' she said clearly and firmly. 'Please, Pauline. Please let me be the chief investigator. I swear I'll always be frearless and never give away any secrets.'

That 'frearless' made Weener smile, but Pauline did not seem to notice it. 'It's a pretty dangerous position, you know,' she told Verity sternly. 'It'll mean shadowing people; in the middle of the night sometimes. You'll have to go through people's letters, look for clues, take terrible risks. And it won't be any good running to Eva, you know, because if you ask me, that woman's just about as fishy as her rotten mother.'

Verity's eyes bulged with excitement. 'I won't. Honestly I won't,' she said earnestly. 'Oh gosh, Pauline, thank you ever so much.'

She threw her arms around Pauline's waist and held her close. Pauline pushed her away. 'And you can cut out all that mucky stuff,' she said crisply. 'I'm your captain now, you know. For your own safety, you must do everything I tell you to and always show me respect.'

Verity nodded solemnly.

'What do vice-captains do, Pauline?' Weener asked, hoping the job would be as exciting and dangerous as Verity's.

Pauline scratched her head and looked thoughtful, then she stopped and gazed back along the road. Weener followed the direction of her glance and saw they had come quite a long way and the cottage now looked small, almost insignificant against the skyline.

'Well,' Pauline said at last, 'we're not likely to find out anything standing around here. I think you'd better go back to the house and ask if we can come in now.'

Weener felt cheated. It seemed terribly unfair that she should have to face Frau Königsberg all on her own; particularly as the answer would undoubtedly be 'no'.

'I know it's a dangerous mission, Weener,' Pauline said quickly. 'Goodness knows what you might find there, but you did promise to be fearless, you know. And being vice-captain means you've got to set a good example to Verity.'

Weener suddenly realized Pauline was asking her to do something very important. It was no good carping about being frightened of Frau Königsberg because she was a murderer. It was no good whining that it was a long way to go just to get the wrong answer. There might be something fishy going on in the cottage and she was going to be the one to find out what it was. She pulled herself up and saluted smartly. 'Aye aye, Captain.' she said.

Pauline smiled briefly. 'While you're gone, Verity and I will work out a few rules and codes and things.'

Weener smiled to herself as she turned and started to trot back down the road. It was just as well she had accepted the mission. Working out rules and codes sounded terribly boring.

'Good luck,' Pauline shouted after her. 'And keep your head down.'

Weener obediently pulled her neck down into her shoulders so that her chin was tucked down on her chest. It was very uncomfortable, which was probably why she did not notice the frozen puddle in front of her. Suddenly, her feet slipped and pitched her forward onto her knees. At first, her legs were too cold to let her feel anything, but as she stood up, she noticed that one of her knees hurt dreadfully. She looked down and saw that the rough ice had not only torn a big hole in her stocking, it had taken most of the skin from her knee as well.

'What on earth are you doing?' Pauline called crossly.

Weener bit her lip as she searched through her pocket. 'Cut my knee,' she called back heroically. 'It's all right though. I've got a hanky.'

'Well, for goodness sake, hurry up,' Pauline snapped. Weener tied the handkerchief around her knee and limped on down the road.

She had a good scout round before she quietly let herself in through the gate, but there was nobody there to see her. Keeping her head well down, she crept up to the kitchen window and cautiously peered in.

Frau Königsberg and Eva were sitting on either side of the kitchen table with a pile of untidy papers between them. Neither of them noticed Weener, but in the elbow-chair at the head of the table, a man sat staring at the window with pale, unblinking eyes. He wore a thick, grey coat which was steaming faintly from the heat of the stove behind him. His hair was pale; his face grey and expressionless.

Weener recognised him immediately. He was the man she had seen with her mind's eye that day when Eva told her about the dead men on the train. It was Kurt sitting there. It was Kurt with his dead, unseeing eyes.

She felt her jaw drop and then go rigid. She felt her eyes stretch open so wide that it felt her eyeballs must drop out. But she was powerless to move and, as she unwillingly watched, the ghost stood up, walked over to the far wall and disappeared into a patch of darkness.

Suddenly Eva was with her. 'What are you doing, you naughty girl? I said you were to stay outside and play with the sisters.'

'Kurt,' Weener moved her jaw with difficulty. 'Eva, I've just seen your brother, Kurt.'

Eva made a funny noise at the back of her throat and, for a moment, she seemed to be as frightened as Weener. She rubbed her hand over her face and then looked down. 'This we must look into,' she said decisively. 'If you have seen him, then you have seen a ghost, for my poor brother died more than a month ago.'

She took Weener by the hand and led her into the kitchen.

Weener pointed to the far wall. 'There,' she said in a hoarse whisper. 'That's where he disappeared.'

71

Eva led her across the room and stopped by a rough wooden door. 'And this was where he disappeared?' she asked, and, when Weener nodded her agreement, she quickly went on, 'Then if it was not a ghost, he will still be in there. It is the larder, you see.' Weener nodded. She was not in the least afraid of Eva opening the door because she knew instinctively the ghost would not be there. Eva seemed to be frightened though, because she muttered what sounded like a spell in German before she flung the door open.

There was nothing to see in the half-light but sacks of potatoes and Frau Königsberg's storage jars neatly arranged in rows on the shelves.

'It must have been a ghost,' Weener told her. 'I saw him first sitting at the table with you and you didn't see him at all, did you?'

Eva sighed and shook her head sadly. 'No, but I wish I had. I loved him so much *Liebchen*, that even though he is dead, I would have liked to see him just once more.'

Weener squeezed her hand. 'Poor Eva,' she murmured.

From the other side of the room, Frau Königsberg rapped out some orders in German. Eva looked down at the blood-stained handkerchief around Weener's knee and gasped.

'My poor darling is hurt,' she breathed, as she picked Weener up and carried her over to the table. 'We must bathe you and make you all better.'

And she made such a lovely fuss of Weener's damaged knee that Weener forgot all about the secret society and that she was supposed to be asking if Pauline and Verity could come in now.

XI
The picture

For supper that evening they had a strange green soup with fluffy white lumps floating on the surface. As they came to the table to eat it, Frau Königsberg threw up her hands in horror, then had a loud German quarrel with Eva. There was silence for some minutes before she stomped over to the dresser and brought out three white cloths which she tied around their waists.

'I'm not wearing an apron!' Pauline said indignantly. 'Tell your mother I am not a baby, Eva.'

She started to untie the cloth, but Frau Königsberg smacked her on the head with a wooden spoon and after wearily raising her eyebrows, Pauline gave in.

There was not really enough to eat. None of them said anything, but it was clear they were still hungry. Frau Königsberg took it as an insult; Eva, as a grievous wound.

'I should never have brought you,' she kept saying as they washed and got ready for bed.

She unrolled a thin, flock mattress and laid it on a broad wooden shelf in the corner of the kitchen. She fetched sheets, pillows and a big continental quilt from some remote corner of the cottage, then covered the mattress with them until it looked quite like a bed. The girls watched in amazement.

'To bed.' she told them when she had finished.

'On that?' Pauline asked in horror.

'Of course on that.'

'What, all together?'

'Of course all together.'

'Good heavens!'

'Where will you be, Eva?' Verity asked as they fidgeted themselves into a straight row on the shelf.

Eva kissed her. 'I shall be in the front room with my mother, but do not worry, *Liebling*. On a good German bed, you will all sleep like little angels.'

As it turned out, she was wrong. Weener, who was in the middle, was wide awake. She told them about the ghost, and that woke Pauline and Verity up too.

'And did he really just vanish?' Verity asked excitedly. Weener nodded in the dark.

'I don't believe you.' Pauline said reassuringly.

'It's true, honestly.'

'And didn't they see him?' Verity asked.

'No. Not everyone can see ghosts, you know.'

Pauline was silent for some moments. 'You had your eyes open? It wasn't like when you look at your Dreamer?'

'I had my eyes open all the time. Cross my heart.'

'Then we'd better get to the bottom of this. Vety, go and have a listen at their door.'

'Why me?' Verity had just begun to get warm and comfortable.

'Because you're the chief investigator. Go on, you joined the secret society and I'm the captain. I order you to go.'

Verity sighed and rolled out of bed. She padded across the cold flagstones, wincing at every step, then stopped by the door and looked back. Pauline was half-sitting up, resting on one elbow.

'Go on.' she hissed.

Verity sighed and obeyed.

It was very dark in the passageway and bitterly cold. As she crept up to the door of the front room and put her ear to the keyhole, Verity could not help wishing Pauline had never thought of the secret society. She was sure that Eva and her mother would not be doing anything fishy in there. Still, she had agreed to be the chief investigator, so she dutifully took up her post and listened.

The voices rose and fell as Frau Königsberg scolded and

74

Eva placated. Verity could not understand all that was being said and none of it sounded very important. Her feet were aching and the cold seemed to be travelling in waves right up her legs to her bottom. A clock behind the door struck eight and suddenly Verity decided that it was much too late for her to be out of bed, so she crept back down the corridor and let herself quietly into the kitchen.

'Well?' Pauline asked as she clambered back onto the shelf.

'Oh, it was only boring grown-ups talk.'

'Ow!' Weener shouted. 'Get your beastly cold feet out of the way.'

'Be quiet,' Pauline told her importantly. 'Come on, Vety, tell us everything you heard.'

'Well,' Verity's voice came out shakily because she was shivering and her teeth were chattering. 'Frau Königsberg said, "God took away my good sons and left me a fool for a daughter". Then Eva said, "I had to bring them. The mother was going away. I could not ask for more leave".'

'Of all the cheek,' Weener whispered indignantly. 'I never knew she was going away.'

'Oh, shut up, Weener. Go on, Vety,' Pauline said encouragingly.

'Well, then Frau Königsberg said, "The little girl will talk and we will be damaged", and Eva said, "She is a child who sees ghosts": at least, I think that's what she meant. I should think a "*Geist*" was a ghost, wouldn't you, Weener?'

'What then?' Pauline asked excitedly.

'Well, I thought it was all pretty unimportant stuff, so I came back.'

'Pretty unimportant!' Pauline's voice was loud with scornful indignation. 'This is vital information. Go back and have another listen.'

'It's ever so cold.' Verity pleaded.

'Stop whining. If you don't go, I'll never let you be in the secret society again.'

Verity took one minute more of glorious warmth and

then got out of bed. She padded up to her listening post and was just about to put her ear to the keyhole, when the door suddenly opened in her face and Eva stood before her in the doorway.

'What are you doing out of bed, you naughty girl?'

Verity bit her lip while she thought quickly. 'I just wanted to say something to Frau Königsberg,' she said innocently. 'Please Eva. It's very important.'

Eva pulled her lips down at the corners, as though she guessed Verity was lying. 'All right then. But you must be quick.'

Verity padded across the threshold. It was a pretty room: pale with the light of an oil lamp and full of furniture painted with gaudy flowers. Frau Königsberg was sitting by a little fire clicking her knitting needles angrily together.

'Frau Königsberg,' Verity began bravely, 'I think we might have seemed very rude to you and very ungrateful. We do love it here, and you and Eva. And I think it's very kind of you to share your food with us; especially as you are such an old woman.' She held her pyjama trousers out at the knee and did the little curtsey that Eva had been teaching her.

Eva knelt down beside her and held her very close. 'Oh, my little angel!' she gasped, then looking up at Frau Königsberg, she went on in German, 'Mummy, Mummy, here is a little angel.' She quickly translated what Verity had said and, after a moment, the deep folds of Frau Königsberg's face lifted into a smile of radiant beauty. She held out her arms and, without a moment's hesitation, Verity ran to her. She scrambled up onto the welcoming lap and the arms folded around her. Frau Königsberg rocked her backwards and forwards while she murmured words of love into her hair. When it was over, she sat back and asked Verity a question in German.

'She wants to know why you could not sleep,' Eva said.

'Because I was sorry,' Verity lied. 'And because I was missing Goldie.' That bit, anyway, was true.

Eva's eyes moistened and her expression melted as she

murmured, 'Little angel, little angel, come down from heaven.' She turned to Frau Königsberg. 'Her dog,' she said in German that Verity could understand. 'She is lonely for her little dog.'

Verity began to feel uncomfortable as a part of her mind told her she was being a terrible crawler. 'Well, he's not really my dog. He belongs to Pauline, but I love him just the same.' The words came out in German although she had not been expecting it.

Frau Königsberg's face swooped on her and planted a big, floppy kiss on her cheek. She set Verity down, then stood up and lifted a picture from the chimney-breast. She held it out to Verity. 'A little angel for a little angel.' she murmured.

Verity looked at it and smiled. It was a portrait of a plump little girl with frizzy golden hair and an armful of fat, pink roses.

'For you,' Eva said encouragingly.

Verity felt a cheat, and it was all so emotional, that her eyes filled tears. But just as the women began to gasp and kiss her again, a series of heavy footsteps sounded on the ceiling above them. They all looked up in silence.

'What was that?' Verity whispered after a few moments.

Eva picked her up. 'The wind, *Liebling*: only the wind.' She carried her over to the doorway. 'Say goodnight.'

'Goodnight, dear Frau Königsberg,' Verity called, then, hating herself, she blew a kiss.

'You really are a little worm,' Pauline told Verity, once she had been settled back into bed and Eva had returned to the front room. 'You know just how to make grown-ups do anything you want them to.'

Verity felt like crying, but she fought it back. 'Well, anyway, I did find out one thing. There is a ghost. I heard him walking upstairs, so I'm not so stupid, am I?'

'I don't believe you.' Pauline said scornfully.

'I *did*.' Verity countered, then turned over and closed her eyes. She wished she did not know how to be sweet. She wished she did not have that thing inside her which told her with unnerving accuracy, just how to make people love her. The trouble was, she could never resist doing it, because she needed so badly to be loved.

XII
Goldie

When they got home, Eva hung Verity's picture in the nursery. 'Oh, we haven't really got to look at that awful mug every day of our lives, have we?' Pauline groaned.

'Perhaps it will teach you how to be good like your little sister,' Eva reproved as she stood back to admire her work.

'She looks as if she's about to say, "I love my Mummy and my Daddy and the little Lord Jesus asleep in the hay",' Weener muttered, and then just to remind everybody that she did actually exist, she said loudly, 'Ow! My knee doesn't half hurt.'

But Verity loved the picture and thought it looked really beautiful hanging there. She hardly dared to hope that she was as pretty as that.

'I'm going to show it to Goldie,' she shouted as she ran up the little corridor to the drawing-room.

The drawing-room door was half open and as Verity sidled in, she saw Fritz standing by the drinks trolley.

'Hallo Fritz,' she said to his back, 'where's Goldie?'

He started guiltily and delayed a few seconds before turning to face her. 'Ah, it is the Fräulein Verity.' His gaze seemed to skid past her. 'The father is not yet home.'

'Oh,' Verity paused. 'Actually, it was Goldie I wanted.'

He turned back to the trolley and began to polish the glasses, rubbing carefully down the cut facets so that they twinkled with diamond colours in the late afternoon sunlight.

'I think perhaps the father will bring back many friends, so the glasses must be perfect, yes? And for the mother, I shall make a very special cocktail. You think she will like?'

'Oh,' Verity frowned for a second, 'yes, I expect she will. Do you know where Goldie is?'

He glanced at her briefly, then held one of the glasses up to the light and inspected it with care. 'You must ask the father when he comes home.'

'Why?' Verity asked.

'Because it is he who will tell you.'

'When will he be back?'

Fritz looked at his watch. 'Not for another hour.'

'Oh, I can't wait that long,' Verity said impatiently. 'I've got a picture I want to show to Goldie. I'll go and see if he's in the kitchen.'

'*Fräulein*, wait,' Fritz called after her as she ran out of the front door, but Verity pretended not to hear him.

Goldie was not on the wide gallery that gave on to the main stairway and he was not in any of the reception rooms. Verity called him as she ran through the dining-room, then pushed through the swing doors and into the little corridor that led to the kitchen.

'Where's Goldie, Gretta?' she called to the scullery maid who was peeling potatoes at the sink. Gretta's back stiffened, but she did not turn around.

One of the chefs came up and made shooing movements with his hands.

'Where's Goldie?' Verity asked and when he shrugged uncomprehendingly, she said, '*Mein Hund? Wo ist mein Hund, Goldie?*' The chef shrugged again. '*Verstehe nicht*' he muttered as he turned back to the vast cooking range.

Nobody bothered about her any more as she searched all the likely corners of the kitchen. 'Where is he?' she asked at last, but nobody turned to answer. Verity sighed and went back up the service stairs to their quarters.

Eva was changing Weener's bandage as Verity came into the bedroom. There was a thick, brown scab over where the graze had been. Eva looked up.

'Ah, you see how quickly it has healed? Soon the scab will come off and then there will be no scar at all.'

'Does it hurt?' Verity asked.

'No. It itches right down to the middle of my knee.' Weener eyed it menacingly. 'I could really give it a good scratch.' Eva laughed and quickly wrapped a fresh bandage around it.

'But this you will not do or it will open up again.'

Weener and Verity shuddered.

'Where have you been, *Liebling*?' Eva asked as she pinned the bandage into place.

'I've been looking for Goldie. I can't find him anywhere.'

'Oh, he has probably gone for a little walk.' Eva patted Weener's head, 'There, now you can do up your stocking, *Liebchen*.'

'Can I go and look for him, please?' Verity asked.

Eva pulled a doubtful face and then gave in. 'You can go just as far as the trees.'

'Promise faithfully and cross my heart.' Verity answered automatically as she pulled on her coat. Without waiting to button it up, she ran back down the service stairs and out into the grounds.

Most of the snow had melted while they had been away. The grass, now laid bare, was rough and tufted under her feet.

Right up until the time that she reached the trees, Verity had every intention of keeping her promise, but Goldie was nowhere to be found and dusk was beginning to gather. She went a little way down the path, then stopped and called him. There was no reply, only the rustle of the birds going to roost.

An awful thought suddenly hit her: suppose he had thought when he was left alone that they did not want him any more? Suppose he had joined the wild dogs in the forest?

She called again and somehow her feet were impelled down the path towards the shooting-lodge. She knew she was being naughty and she knew also that she was getting frightened, but she kept expecting to see Goldie come running out to meet her.

81

The light was fading fast and the forest seemed to be wrapped in a heavy stillness. The tall trees lowered down at her. It seemed they were silent only because they were holding some terrible secret. The sound of her feet pattering on the path seemed suddenly dangerous and instinctively she moved closer to the forest and trod more quietly.

She reached the bend in the path and, on an impulse, she ducked into the forest and hid behind a tree, then stood for some moments with her eyes tightly closed while she fought to stop her heart from hammering.

A slight noise made her catch her breath and press herself closer to the tree for protection. She bit her lip and made herself peer around the trunk.

Kurt's ghost was standing motionless on the path: his pale eyes staring in the direction of the Kaiserhof. He had a cigarette hanging loosely from the corner of his lifeless lips and his grey coat rested casually on his shoulders.

Verity screwed up her eyes and pressed her face against the hard bark of the tree. 'Fairies, pixies, elves,' she said with the voice of her mind. 'Ghosts can't hurt you. They can only give you a fright.' The spell worked because, when she looked again, the ghost had gone. She waited until her legs had stopped shaking, then ran through the trees to the clearing by the river. 'Goldie!' she called. 'Goldie!' She paused and listened to the river rippling against the silence. An owl hooted and was answered by another owl. Verity called again and then begged, 'Oh please come back, please. I love you so much.'

A ghost laughed: a hard, nasty laugh which seemed to come from the bushes at her side. Verity felt the blood drain from her head so that she was light and dizzy with fear.

Suddenly she was running and now the forest was not silent any more. It was filled with the noise of her hammering heart, her gasping breath and the heavy pounding footsteps that were following her.

As she ran, dusk turned to night and the black path, the black sky and the black trees around her seemed to swallow

82

her in a tide of panic. Once, she thought the ghost was about to catch her, but something in her pushed her to even greater speed so that she seemed to be almost flying as she broke out of the forest and into the grounds of the Kaiserhof. Then, quite suddenly, her legs buckled beneath her and she collapsed on to the brittle, freezing grass.

She heard footsteps coming towards her, but she could not get up. She could not even shrink away as a hand caught hold of her shoulder.

'What do you do, little girl?' a man's voice asked.

'I want Goldie.' Verity wailed.

The man said something that she could not understand. He lifted her from the ground. 'Look at me,' he said.

Verity shook her head. 'You're only a ghost. I don't believe in ghosts, so there.'

The man laughed. 'I am not a ghost. I am the guard.'

Verity opened her eyes and saw that it was true. 'Oh,' she gasped as she threw her arms around his neck. 'Thank you for saving me.'

He laughed again as he stooped lopsidedly and picked up his rifle. 'You are hurt?' he asked.

Verity shook her head. 'A ghost chased me all the way through the forest, but I got away. Are you German?' she added.

The guard's face went blank, then he turned away and spat at the grass. 'I am Czech.' he said bitterly. He carried Verity in silence to the front door, then set her down and patted her head. 'No more into the forest, please.' he said reprovingly then, shouldering his rifle, he marched off into the night.

Verity did not want to run the risk of meeting up with Eva, so she went up the front stairs to their quarters.

The door to the drawing-room was open and a welcoming yellow light spilled out into the little corridor. She took off her coat and folded it into a tidy bundle so her mother would not guess what she had been doing, then wandered

83

casually into the drawing-room with the bundle under her arm.

'Mummy,' she started, and then stopped as she saw her father sitting in the armchair beside the fire. 'Oh, I'm sorry, Daddy. I didn't mean to disturb you.'

He made an angry noise beneath his moustache. 'Now, why would you think I wouldn't want to see you, Verity. You're my little girl. You can come and talk to me whenever you like. I mean, don't you think it's about time we got to know each other?' Verity nodded enthusiastically.

She dumped her coat on the settee, then ran to him and clambered on to his knee. 'We do all love you, Daddy,' she lied as she snuggled against him. He laughed and tweaked her hair. 'D'ya, you soppy little flirt? I bet you say that to all the boys.'

Verity giggled obligingly then stared in silence at the fire. 'Daddy, where's Goldie?' she asked at last.

He scratched the corner of his moustache thoughtfully and then he said, 'I'm afraid poor old Goldie's dead, poppet.' Verity blinked and stared up at him, noticing for the first time that he had slanting, grey eyes, just like Weener's.

'You're teasing me.' she told him decidedly.

He sighed. 'I wish I were, poppet.'

'Well, what did he die of, then?'

Her father ruffled her hair, then squeezed her shoulder. 'Better for you not to know. He was a pretty old dog, you know.'

'He isn't,' Verity countered. 'It's just that the man who had him before us let him get lazy and fat. Eva and I have been taking him for walks and he's ever so much better. Where is he, Daddy? Please don't tease me.'

Her father looked at her and shook his head. 'I'm sorry, poppet, but he's dead.'

A shadow crept across Verity's mind. 'But he can't be. He wasn't ill. He couldn't suddenly die: not just like that. Did someone murder him?'

Her father nodded. ' 'Fraid so.'

'But why? He never hurt anyone. He never did anything that was naughty. He was the best dog in the world. Who murdered him?' He held her closer so that her face was pressed against the prickly material of his uniform. She looked at the little row of ribbons over his top pocket while he gave his version of an answer.

'Well, my sweetie,' he said, 'it's about time you learned that there are two sorts of people here: good Germans and bad Germans. Now the good Germans — like Eva and Fritz for instance — they know the war's over and that we won. They've made their adjustments so they can begin to rebuild their lives. But the bad Germans won't accept, you see, so they're filled with hatred and bitterness. It makes them do horrible things, like what they did to poor old Goldie.'

'What did they do?' Verity asked quietly.

'Better for you not to know, poppet.'

'But I want to know.'

She waited through the ensuing silence, until it was clear he was not going to answer. 'I expect it was Wolfgang,' she said to open the conversation again. 'He had a knife, you know, and he was always going around killing people. I expect it was him, Daddy. Did he kill Goldie with his knife, Daddy?'

'No, poppet.'

'Oh, I suppose he shot him then, or dropped a bomb on him.'

'None of that, sweetie. If you must know, he hit him with a stick.'

Verity laughed because now she knew her father was lying. 'You can't die from being hit with stick. Don't be so soppy, Daddy.'

'If you're hit hard enough and often enough, I'm afraid you can.'

Verity said in a small voice, 'Oh I see,' and as the realization grew in her mind, her body went cold and clammy while goosepimples tickled the back of her scalp.

'I'm going to get you another dog, darling,' he said quickly. 'A little black puppy, just for you and you can take him for walks and teach him tricks. What shall we call him, do you think?'

'No!' Verity's voice was involuntary; almost hysterical. 'You mustn't! Please, please don't! It isn't safe for dogs in Germany.' She scrambled down from his knee. 'I've got to go now.' she said thickly as she stumbled out of the room.

Weener and Pauline were playing snakes and ladders in front of the nursery fire. Weener looked up as Verity came in. 'Did you find him?' she asked.

Verity shook her head. 'He's dead.' she answered thickly.

Weener looked quickly back at the board. 'Hey,' she said indignantly, 'I saw that. You cheated, Pauline. You were on the snake's head. You've got to go down to the bottom.'

'I was not!'

'Yes you were. You cheated!'

'I didn't!'

'He was hit with a stick until he was dead. Wolfgang did it.' Verity looked at the empty patch beneath the radiator. 'He killed Goldie because he hates the English.'

Pauline looked up. 'Of course he didn't,' she said scornfully. 'Crumbs, that dog was as old as the hills. They're like people, you know. They die when they get old and useless like that.'

Something unbearable swelled in Verity's chest, making it impossible for her to be with her sisters any more. She went through to the bedroom and lay down on her bed. She could not cry: she could not even think of Goldie. There was nothing in her but a blank, blind knot of misery which tightened and tightened and ached inside her chest.

XIII
Hitler

That night, Verity found it unbearable to be in bed. The frowsty blanket of darkness in the room oppressed her, while the sound and feeling of her sleeping sisters filled her with a mixture of guilt and irritation. She was acutely aware that the night was ebbing away and that she had no business to be still awake. She longed to sleep, but just as painfully, she longed for someone to talk to. The knot in her throat and chest begged for some release, but the few tears she managed to shed seemed inadequate and only intensified her feeling of guilt.

At last she got up and crept through to the nursery. The light was pale in here. Somehow, it was never properly dark, except in the bedroom where the curtains were thick.

She pulled the little wicker chair up to the radiator, unconsciously placing it by Goldie's favourite spot, and then sat down with her knees drawn up against her chest.

Outside in the grounds, a soldier was crooning a love song in a voice slurred with drink, which sometimes rose above and sometimes was swamped by the distant roar of traffic and the bustle of grown-ups enjoying themselves.

Verity closed her eyes and tried to let her mind concentrate on a feeling of unimportance and inadequacy. There was a certain comfort in this, because a person who was of no account could not be as guilty as she was feeling now. She had always been aware of a sense of failure for having been born a girl. In her logical mind she knew that anybody who already had two little girls could not possibly want a third. She knew that had she been a boy, her father would have been much more interested in his children. She was aware too, that she had been born at a very unsuitable time. All through her life, grown-ups had regarded her with a certain pitying accusation. 'Your poor mother!' they would breathe, 'imagine having to cope with the three of you! And with a war going on too.' Verity knew that if there had been only two children, life would have been much easier for her mother. The strange thing was that her mother did love her and even made a bit of a favourite of her, although this was always hotly denied in public. Verity was endlessly grateful and tried to do everything in her power to compensate for her sex and her poor sense of timing.

But, thinking over these things tonight did not seem to help; in fact, it seemed only to increase her depression. She pushed her head hard against her knees and gritted her teeth against her misery.

She did not hear the click as the nursery door opened, only the faint rustle as Eva knelt down beside her. '*Liebling*,' she murmured. '*Liebling*, I know you hurt.'

Verity looked up. The tenderness in Eva's face released the tight cords that had held her through the night and all the tears that should have been shed earlier, suddenly poured from her eyes.

'Eva, Eva,' she sobbed, 'I wish I wasn't so stupid.'

The statement summed up everything she felt so that once it had been made, she felt better and could relax, sobbing in Eva's arms. Eva let her cry for some moments, then tweaked the hair at the back of her head so that she was forced to look up.

'Stupid?' Eva's face and voice were fierce with mock anger. 'Who tells you you are stupid? I think you are very clever.'

'I didn't mean that sort of stupid,' Verity struggled against her tears to explain. 'I meant "stupid girl" — "stupid English".'

Eva held her close again. 'Sh shhh,' she murmured. 'You will wake the sisters,' and then, while Verity struggled to control herself, she went on, 'and you see, I know. I know

88

why you say you do not want to be English. It is the sisters. They hurt you with their coldness about the little dog. And the mother and the father did not come to your room tonight to comfort you. It is the coldness of the English that makes you so sad.'

Verity rubbed her hand over her eyes. Eva had got it all wrong again. If Verity had been a boy, nobody would have dared to kill Goldie because she would have been able to go out and fight them; and if she had not been English, nobody would have wanted to kill him anyway. But these feelings were too personal and too profound to bring into the open so she let Eva brush the tears away and take her by the hand.

'Come,' Eva's voice was warm and excited. 'Come, I have a little secret I want to share with you.'

None of the girls ever went to Eva's room. It was not because they were not allowed in there; it was more of an unwritten agreement between them and their nursemaid that she should have some privacy. Verity appreciated the compliment of being invited and she was mildly interested in the secret, so she let Eva lead her across the threshold and sit her down on the hard little bed.

'And now,' Eva said as she quietly closed the door, 'and now, I will tell.' She crossed the room and sat down beside Verity. 'Everybody here, do you know what they all say?'

Verity shook her head.

'They all say, "That Fräulein Verity, she cannot be English. She who is so good and gentle, with all that golden hair. That Fräulein Verity", they say, "she must be a little bit German, if not German altogether".'

Verity blinked. She had the feeling of having been suddenly lifted out of her state of nonentity and admitted to a very exclusive club.

'But Eva,' she said, fighting to hold on to mundane reality, 'what about the mother and Daddy and Pauline and Weener? They're all English, so how could I be German?'

Eva laughed and nudged her conspiratorially. 'There were a lot of good German boys in English prisons when you were born, *Liebling*.' Verity did not understand, so she said, 'Oh', darkly, and raised her eyebrows.

Eva laughed and cuddled her. 'I know you do not understand, Fräulein mouse, but believe me, it is possible you are a little bit German and as for me, I shall always believe that it is so.'

Verity gazed at her incredulously for some minutes, then, suddenly throwing caution to the wind, she hugged Eva as closely as she could and whispered, 'Oh, thank you, thank you, Eva.'

'There, you see,' Eva sounded triumphant, 'if you were English, you would not want to be German, would you?'

Verity nodded. 'No, of course I wouldn't. But we'd better not tell the others.'

'It is as I said at the beginning: it is a secret, a special secret between me and you.'

Verity's chest swelled with pride. 'Gosh,' she breathed excitedly.

Eva turned away and began to unfasten her dress. 'Tonight,' she said over her shoulder, 'tonight you will sleep with me. No little German girl has to sleep on her own when she is sad.' She pulled the dress up over her head, then quickly removed her underclothes. Verity gazed with amazement at Eva's huge, pink body which seemed to be loosely made of pink blancmanges. There was a tuft of bright yellow whiskers between Eva's legs which riveted Verity's attention. Eva saw her looking and flipped one of her breasts unceremoniously. 'Big, huh?' she said, then pulled her nightgown over her head.

Verity nodded as Eva's face emerged from the stiff white cotton. 'Excuse me,' she asked diffidently, 'but what are all those whiskers for?'

Eva pulled up her nightgown and pointed to them. 'These?'

Verity nodded.

'All women have these. You have never seen a woman

before?' there was a note of shock in her voice.

'Once,' Verity confided, 'when I went into the wrong room when we first got here. But I only saw her bottom and her wobbledybops.' Eva laughed and jumped into bed. 'Wobbledybops! What funny words you have. Come. Come to bed, mouseling, I have a story I shall tell.'

Verity turned out the light, then climbed into bed beside Eva. 'So, you have never seen even a woman with no clothes on,' Eva said as Verity snuggled down. 'What funny people you are.'

'What about the story?' Verity asked.

'Oh yes, it was when you said you wished you were not a girl. It was funny because when I was just your age I was always thinking the same thing.'

'Girls aren't very important, are they?'

'That is what I thought too. "Who cares about me", was what I used to say, "I am only a girl. Girls are not important". And then, something wonderful happened: so wonderful my life was changed for ever.'

'What?' Verity asked urgently.

'Well, it was like this. My brother was at the university, and because of this, he used to stay with my auntie in the town.'

'Was that Kurt?'

'No. No, Kurt was much younger. This was my big, big brother. He was so handsome and we were so proud. So, one day my mother has a letter. "Come to the town", it said, "and bring little Eva and Kurt. I want you should see me in the parade". Well, my mother cried a little and she scolded a little, but we went because she was so very proud of Walter (that was my brother, you see). I remember it was very cold when we got there and all the houses were so big and grey. The streets, they were grey too and so was the sky. At first I was a little frightened and very sad but then, as we walked along, I saw that somebody had put up pictures. Big pictures with beautiful colours: so it seemed they almost came jumping down from the walls. So I asked my brother, "Who is it who has given us those beautiful pictures to look at?" And do you know what he told me?'

Verity shook her head in the dark.

'He said, "It is Hitler who has given them as he will give everything to the German people".'

Verity bit her lip. She did not want to spoil the story by starting a quarrel about Hitler.

'Well,' Eva went on after a pause, 'the next day, all the pictures had been changed and now they were even bigger, even better, even more beautiful and when I saw them, I began to cry.'

'Why did you cry, Eva?'

Eva laughed in the dark. 'That is what they all said to me, "Why do you cry, Eva?" So I told them it was the pictures. You see, they were all of a little girl, looking so happy and so healthy and on the picture it said, "*Alle Zehnjährigen zu uns*". Do you know what that mean, *Liebchen*?'

Verity shook her head again.

'It means, "Every ten-year-old to us". And to me, it meant that Hitler loved little girls and he didn't think that they were not important. He wanted little girls in his party because he loved them as much as all his German people. It was so wonderful for me to know that, and yet I cried because I did not understand just how good and wonderful he was. The picture said, "Every ten-year-old" and, like you are now, I was only six. Well, when I told my brother, Walter, why I was crying, he was very grave and then, quite suddenly, he went off and left us. I thought that I had made him angry; but no. That evening, when he came home, he had wonderful news. He had told the party how I loved the Führer and how I had cried because I was only six and they said, because I was such a good German, I could give the flowers to the Führer at the parade.'

Verity gasped with envy. 'And did you, Eva?' she asked excitedly.

'Oh yes!' Eva's voice was radiant in the darkness. 'I had a beautiful white dress and white socks and shoes and I walked up in front of all those lines of people and gave my flowers to the Führer. He kissed me and then quietly he told me that all little girls were important and I must never think that he didn't love or want me again.'

Verity lay for some moments, basking in the reflected glory of Eva's triumph. 'I wish I could have done that,' she said at last.

'Well, who knows, perhaps one day you will.'

'But Hitler's dead, Eva.'

She laughed and held Verity closer. 'Hitler isn't dead, mouseling. They could not kill our Führer: he, who was so strong and loved all his people so much! No, he waits in the Black Forest and one day, who knows, it could be quite soon now, he will rise up and he will lead his glorious German people to victory.'

'Gosh!' Verity gasped incredulously.

'And when that day comes, who knows, it might be you who is chosen to give the flowers.'

'Oh, but Eva —' Verity began, but Eva interrupted her with a kiss.

'Already we have said you are a little bit German, so why should it not be you? We shall have to get you ready, I think. We could not let the Führer see you in those horrible brown stockings. Tomorrow, I will start to knit you socks: lovely white socks like the ones I wore on that wonderful day.'

'Really?' Verity asked incredulously.

'Of course, really.'

Verity was quiet for some minutes and then she said reluctantly, 'Eva, I don't want to spoil everything, but Hitler wasn't always good, was he? I mean, he did do some naughty things.'

'Naughty things!' Eva demanded indignantly. 'What naughty things?'

'Well, he did go around killing people, didn't he?' Verity struggled to keep her voice conciliatory.

'Lies!' Eva answered angrily. 'All lies!'

'Well, he did kill all the Pringles, you know. Honestly, he dropped a bomb on them.'

There was silence for some moments and then Eva's voice swamped the room with bitterness. 'One day, I hope you will go to Dresden: perhaps one day to Hamburg too! And you talk to me of a few dead Pringles!'

'I'm sorry.'

Eva was quiet again and then she asked in a more gentle voice, 'What is this — this Pringle?'

'Oh,' Verity was careful to keep her tone casual, 'they were just some people and they did live very close to the railway station, you know.'

'There you are, then.' Eva was confident again. 'Now, you must go to sleep, or you will never be chosen to give the flowers to the Führer.'

And Verity, closing her eyes, found it very easy to obey.

XIV
Kurt's ghost

In the weeks that followed Goldie's death, Weener was aware of a confusing change in both her sisters. Now, it was Verity who seemed to hold herself aloof and had that distant air of importance and superiority that Weener had always associated with Pauline. Eva was mainly responsible. In the past she had protected and sided with Verity, but now she openly set her above the other two. Weener agreed with the treatment to begin with: Verity had been so very unhappy about Goldie dying. But, as the weeks went on, she began to resent the favouritism and to become increasingly frightened of what it was doing.

Pauline was jealous and her jealousy was making her peculiar and completely terrifying. Weener was used to her sister being bossy and sometimes even hitting people if they stepped out of line. She could accept that because Pauline was the eldest, but she could not cope with the way Pauline had begun to behave. It was almost as if she deliberately worked herself into a rage so that she could attack blindly and callously without any fear of reprisals.

At first, Eva was her target. She would run at her for no apparent reason, kicking and hitting as hard as she could. Eva, who was so much bigger and stronger, never had any problem in getting the better of these attacks and, once Pauline had been slapped and shaken, she would be dragged roughly by the arm until she was face to face with Verity's picture.

'Black witch!' Eva would scream at her. 'There is a little girl. That is what a little girl looks like. Do you look like that? No, you do not because I will tell you why. You are not a little girl. You are a black devil come from hell!' Then she would make Pauline stand in front of the picture for at least an hour because, she said, the devil hated to look on goodness so it was a fitting punishment.

The picture had begun to dominate all their lives. Pauline hated it, Weener dreaded it, and Verity began to look more like it every day. She held her head a little to one side now and when she smiled, it was the same simpering, vapid expression. Often, when Eva saw her doing it, she would sweep her up and cuddle her, then say to the other two, 'See, here is my little angel.' Even Weener found this revolting and she wished Eva would not do it because it was making Pauline hate Verity.

Soon, it was Verity, not Eva, who became the object of Pauline's terrifying attacks. It hurt and frightened Weener to be so powerless to help. She began to hate Eva for goading Pauline. She began to hate Pauline for attacking Verity and, against her will, she began to hate and despise Verity for simply being there and causing all the trouble.

The secret society had ceased to exist from the moment they all returned to the Kaiserhof, and it was a particularly difficult time because she had been trying very hard not to see her Dreamer any more. She agreed with her mother that she was too old to go on seeing him and, anyway, she was still angry with him about her hair. Although it had grown quite a bit since the comb incident, it was still not long enough to plait and, with it loose, she sometimes looked very like Verity.

For his part, the Dreamer did everything he could to get back in favour with her, but it was not until he agreed to stop being mysterious, that Weener finally forgave him. She was amazed to find that he was really a very nice person. His name was Lord Shonkerdinkle and he had been swindled out of all his money by his uncle. He had two little girls, Beaulah and Beatrix, who were always glad to play with Weener. Lady Shonkerdinkle was frail and spent most of her time cleaning their enormous castle with a brightly coloured feather duster. Weener sometimes had to carry the duster for her because Lady Shonkerdinkle was often ill. 'Not long for this world', was her husband's verdict. Weener had promised she would marry him and bring up his two little girls as if they were her own just as soon as his wife died. The whole family was very happy about the arrangement and, in fact, she was already known to all of them as Lady Weener Shonkerdinkle. It was a source of constant amazement to her that she had known the Dreamer for so long and never realized what a kind and polite man he really was. He never called her 'old girl' now and he never sang rude songs. She was sure that if her mother knew the change that had come over him, she would be only too happy to know that Weener often went to his castle now and was planning to marry him.

Because of this new relationship, Weener was annoyed when she was told that she, Pauline and Verity would be going with Eva to stay at the little house in the forest. It seemed so pointless because their father had been posted and they would all be moving away from the Kaiserhof in just a week's time. She asked the Shonkerdinkles if they would like to come too, but Lady Shonkerdinkle was ill again and the family was much too loyal to go away and leave her on her own.

Weener had begged to be allowed to stay behind, but her parents were going away that week-end, so there would be nobody to look after her. She wanted to say she would be fine with the Shonkerdinkles, but she remembered just in time that she was not allowed to make up stories, so she held her tongue and agreed to go.

Pauline was against the visit too, but that was because it was Verity's treat, so nobody took any notice of her.

The forest was very still on that early Spring morning when they all set off. There was a pervading warmth in the pale sun which seemed to draw the delicate scent of earth and pine-needles so that it was all around them.

Pauline was in a bad temper because Eva would not let them go by jeep as their mother had suggested.

'To walk is good for you,' Eva snapped. 'Do you want to grow up pale and flabby like other English women?'

'I thought I wasn't supposed to be human. I thought I was supposed to be a devil.' Pauline said distantly, then instinctively ducked away from Eva's pro-forma slap.

Although their bags were quite heavy, Weener was secretly glad that they were walking: the forest was so enchanting. Once they surprised a little brown rabbit sitting on the path in front of them. It crouched for some seconds; ears back, dark eyes bulging with terror, while they all stood still and watched it. Then suddenly it took a tremendous flying leap into the forest and hopped away, its white tail bobbing in the sunlight.

'We should have caught him,' Weener said wistfully. 'We could have made him into a pet.'

'Or a good rabbit stew.' Eva teased, then laughed darkly at her own wit.

Verity tucked the strap of her bag over her shoulder and began to hop along the path. Just recently, Eva had taken their clothes in hand. She had knitted them all long white socks and taken up the hems of Verity's skirts. The frock she was wearing that day was so short that when she hopped, she showed a big patch of white knickers. It made her look a bit like a rabbit which, in turn, made Weener laugh and hop up to join her.

Verity was grinning her old grin and her eyes twinkled as they used to do. She put her hands under her chin and wiggled her nose. Weener felt a sudden rush of love for her and, putting her free arm around Verity's shoulder, she hopped with her down the path to the little house.

They were hot and out of breath by the time they reached the clearing, but they could not stop giggling. Suddenly everything they did seemed to be funny. They put their bags down on the little verandah in the front of the house and started to hop back to meet Pauline and Eva.

Weener saw their mistake too late. She saw Pauline break out of the forest; her face was taut and white and her eyes glittered with anger. She marched up to Verity and, grabbing her by the hair, swung her away from Weener, then began to punch and kick her with a horrible ferocity. Weener covered her face with her hands and screamed with all the strength in her lungs until above the noise she was making, she heard the familiar shout of, 'Black witch! Black witch from hell!' She knew Pauline was being dragged away, but she did not look up until Eva, as she drew level, shouted at her, 'And you! What use are you? You never try to help your little sister.'

The tirade filled Weener with a sudden and overwhelming sense of guilt. She dropped her hands and stopped screaming. 'But —' she started to say.

Pauline saw her chance and pulled away from Eva, but within a second she was recaptured and dragged into the house.

Weener's legs felt suddenly weak. She sat down on the steps of the verandah and hugged her body tightly as she rocked backwards and forwards. Everything was so unreal that at times like this, she was sure she was making it all up.

Verity came over and sat down close beside her, putting an arm around her shoulder. 'It's all right, Weener. Don't cry. Really, it's all right.' she comforted.

'It's not,' Weener's voice was thick and choking. 'It's all horrible and revolting. Mummy should never have brought us here.'

There was a loud bang from inside the house followed by a roar of anger. Weener took hold of Verity's hand. 'Let's run away.' she said urgently.

Verity shook her head. 'We can't. Don't be daft, Weener. We don't even know where we are, so how would we know where to go to?' Weener had no answer so they sat in silence until they heard the door open behind them and Eva came out onto the verandah carrying a tray with a jug and two glasses on it.

'For two good girls, I have a lemon drink.' She set the tray down on a log table which stood on the verandah. 'Come to the table, please. I have found some special glasses, so perhaps you could play at being grown-ups.'

They both stood up obediently and moved over to the table. 'Oh, what sad faces!' Eva coaxed. 'This is a holiday. You must enjoy yourselves. The witch I have locked in her room.' Weener followed the direction of her glance and saw Pauline's white face hovering in the window above them. It stayed for a second and then it was gone. She felt a catch of sadness in the back of her throat.

'You are safe,' Eva laughed, obviously misunderstanding Weener's expression. 'Sit down, please, and I, the waitress, shall pour out drinks for the ladies.'

The glasses were much too beautiful for children to use. They were long-stemmed goblets with grape-vines engraved around the bowls. Weener eyed them warily, but Verity sat down on the log bench beside the table and took a sip of lemonade as if she had been using glasses like that all her life. 'It's lovely.' she said, putting on her picture smile.

It was all so unreal that Weener felt distanced from them, as though they were a dream she could not escape. 'I've got to be excused.' she muttered as she pushed her way into the house.

She found herself in a small oak-panelled hall which had a steep flight of stairs running from its centre to a bannistered gallery surrounding the first floor. Weener had a sudden feeling that she must find Pauline and talk to her: force her, if necessary, to say what was making her so angry. Somebody, she reasoned as she ran up the stairs, somebody had to make things ordinary again.

She went around the gallery, trying all the doors until she found the one that was locked, then she called softly, 'Pauline, Pauline. It's me, Weener.' There was no answer so she bent down to peer through the keyhole.

Pauline was sitting on her bed, directly opposite the door. She was still very pale and her eyes glittered unnaturally. There was something about the way her fists were clenched and the tension of her body which frightened Weener and made her feel the door was too flimsy to offer any proper protection. She bit her lip while she screwed up her courage to try again. 'I've come to say I want to be friends. Please, Pauline,' she wheedled, 'we've got to go back to being friends again: all of us. It's so horrible like this.'

Pauline's eyes seemed to glare straight through the door at her. 'You stupid twit, Weener.' she said contemptuously before she turned away and moved out of Weener's line of vision.

'Please,' Weener pleaded, 'I could help you.'

'Mind your own damn business.' Pauline's voice was so loaded with controlled hatred that Weener found herself backing away.

She wandered down the gallery and opened the first door she came to. It turned out to be the bathroom so she went in and sat, surrounded by impersonal white tiles, while she tried to work out what had gone wrong.

If only Lord Shonkerdinkle could have come with us, she thought wistfully, he'd know what to do. She looked at the shower curtains directly in front of her and tried to imagine his kind, smiling face. But, instead of Lord Shonkerdinkle, she seemed to see straight through the curtains and the partition wall, directly into Pauline's bedroom. Weener felt suddenly vulnerable and in a blind panic, she ran out of the bathroom, slamming the door behind her. Without stopping to look, but certain she was being pursued, she raced down the stairs, out of the house and onto the verandah.

Eva had gone, but Verity was still sitting at the table, seemingly oblivious of the white face glaring down at her from the upstairs window. 'My deah, you've been an age!' she minced in a voice that was supposed to sound like a grown-up.

Weener went up to her and took her arm. 'Don't let's play that game,' she said urgently. 'Come for a walk with me, Vety.' Verity's face registered surprise, but she stood up willingly. 'OK,' she said as they stepped down from the verandah, 'I don't really like playing grown-ups anyway. I don't ever want to be a grown-up, do you Weener?'

Weener did not answer. She felt irritated by Verity's prattle and irritated with herself for being so frightened for her. Her instinct told her to get Verity away from the view of Pauline's window because she knew that in a funny, oblique way she was taunting Pauline. But the other part of Weener's mind was mildly surprised that she should be bothered.

'Do you know why I don't want to be a grown-up?' Verity went on as they reached the shelter of the trees. Weener shook her head as she pushed Verity into the forest. Verity turned, looking surprised and hurt. 'Ow,' she said petulantly, rubbing her arm. Weener kissed her. 'Sorry,' she consoled as they linked arms. 'Go on. Tell me why you don't want to be grown-up.'

Verity bit her lip and her eyes twinkled. 'Well,' she said as they began to stroll down the path, 'when you're a grown-up, you grow bright yellow whiskers between your legs.'

The relief of tension and the stupidity of the statement made Weener shout and shake with laughter. She sat down with her back against a tree, hugging her aching ribs.

Verity stood, gazing down; her face deadly serious around her twinkling eyes. 'You do, honestly. Bright yellow ones all around your middle. Isn't it *awful*?'

Weener tried to laugh again, but a corner of her mind was becoming convinced. 'Really?' she asked doubtfully.

Verity nodded.

'How do you know?'

'Eva showed me. She said all women have them.' She sat down and snuggled close to Weener. 'Isn't it awful?' she added.

Weener considered it for some moments. It seemed an improbable state of affairs. She tried to visualize the people she knew, but her mind shuddered away. She had never liked Eva very much and now she felt physically repelled by the very thought of her and her yellow whiskers. She pushed Verity's statement around her mind, considering it from every angle. 'All women?' she asked at last, and Verity nodded. 'Well, you loony, we'll be all right then. When we grow up, we'll be ladies.' The clarity of her verdict surprised her. She had not been aware there would be such an easy solution.

Verity looked surprised though. 'Isn't Eva a lady then?' she asked. Weener stood up, dusting the forest from the seat of her skirt. 'Of course not. She's a German.' She felt irritated again by Verity's stupidity. 'Anyway, you shouldn't have looked.' she said reprovingly.

Verity stood up, looking crushed and guilty. 'I couldn't help it. Anyway, she doesn't mind. Germans look at one another without their clothes on all the time.'

That last remark worried Weener. It was hard to be kind and protective to Verity when she was so dirty minded. She wondered momentarily if that was why Pauline hated her so much and so she asked, 'What made Pauline go for you like that?' Verity's face crumpled and she stood still, looking down at the ground, her arms hanging limply on either side of her. Weener felt instantly guilty. She knew that Verity hated talking about Pauline's rages. She knew in her heart of hearts that Verity had probably done nothing to enrage her. She walked back and put an arm around her little sister then, more to calm her own guilt than to give any comfort, she said importantly, 'I must know the truth Vety, if I'm to do anything to help you.'

Verity looked up, her eyes swimming with tears. 'You can't help. She hates me.'

Weener's heart melted and she felt like crying. 'She doesn't Vety. She didn't when we were in England, so why should she now? Don't you remember when we were in England?'

Verity pulled away and began to sob, 'I don't remember. I don't remember anything.'

As Weener watched her, a feeling of total helplessness came over her. 'Well, it was lovely,' she said to reassure herself. 'I mean, Pauline was bossy, but you know, she wasn't like this.

It'll be all right when we go home. Honestly, Vety, you'll see.' Verity bit her lip, then rubbed her face with her hands as if she was washing it. When she looked up again, the tears had gone. 'Sorry,' she said flatly. 'You're probably right. She probably doesn't really hate me. Sorry.'

Weener hugged her shoulder. 'That's all right and you don't have to tell me what made her go for you — that is, if you don't want to.' She knew the effect this would have and a part of her told her she was being mean and cheating. However, the rest of her was too consumed with curiosity to care, so she added nonchalantly, 'Honestly, I don't mind if you want to keep it a secret.'

Verity's fingers crept into her hand and Weener fought against despising her for capitulating so easily. 'She saw my frock.' Verity whispered.

Weener stopped and looked at her in surprise. 'What frock?' she asked.

Verity looked down at the ground, grinding the toe of her sandal into the path. 'You know the white socks Eva made us?'

Weener nodded.

Verity did not look up, but went on as if she took the nod for granted. 'Well, she's making me a white frock to go with them and Pauline saw it this morning and it made her furious.'

'Why?'

'Oh, I don't think she likes me being so friendly with Eva.'

They began to walk on again while Weener thought it over. 'What's Eva making you a frock for?' she asked after they had walked for some moments in silence. Verity did not answer and so, after a pause, she asked the question again, then looked directly into her sister's face. Verity was frowning and she seemed to be undecided about how to answer.

'Go on,' Weener said quickly. 'What's it for?'

'It's a secret.' Verity answered thickly.

'Oh, I see.' Weener let go of her hand and walked on, gambling on the fact that Verity would rather give up her secret than be abandoned. The gamble paid off. Before she had gone very far, she heard Verity's feet come pattering up the path behind her. 'Promise you'll never tell anyone?' Verity's fingers stole around Weener's hand again.

'Cross my heart and hope to die.' The answer was automatic.

'Eva's got a friend. He's ever so important, and when he comes to see her, I'm going to give him some flowers.'

Weener had never heard such a boring secret in her life and she nearly laughed out loud at Verity for fighting so hard to hold on to it. But Verity did not seem to realize what she was thinking. 'Weener,' she asked, 'why don't you talk about your Dreamer any more?'

Weener shrugged. It was a very personal area with her and she did not want to discuss it with Verity.

'Has he gone away, Weener?'

'Of course not.' Weener answered shortly. They were by the river now and she picked up a stone and threw it into the water, watching the bright ripples as they fanned out like a little whirlpool.

'I used to like it when you talked about him. Do you want to talk about him now?'

'No.'

'Why not?'

Weener sat down on the grassy bank and scowled at the water. 'If you must know, because nobody believes me and Mummy says I'm too old to tell silly stories. But they're not silly stories, honestly Vety.' She heard her voice getting excited, in spite of herself, and she had a sudden and urgent need to be believed. 'I do see things. And I really did see Kurt's ghost.'

Verity nodded sympathetically. 'I know. I saw it too. Here in the forest. It chased me all the way home.'

Weener was too excited to be frightened. 'Really?' she asked breathlessly. 'Why didn't you tell anyone?'

Verity looked sadly at the water. 'I don't know.' There was something in her voice that made Weener know she was lying but she was too busy with a new idea to wonder about it.

'Vety,' she asked breathlessly, 'Vety, would you tell Mummy? You know, about you seeing him too?'

'Why?'

'Well, then she'd know I don't just make up stories. Will you, Vety, please?'

Verity beamed at her. 'Of course I will.'

Weener lay back in the grass, basking in the wave of relief that swept over her. 'Oh gosh,' she said. 'Oh gosh, Vety. We should always be friends and stick together. Promise me. Promise me faithfully that you'll tell her.'

Verity sat down beside her and promised again and again. Listening with her eyes half closed, Weener forgot her sister's faults and began to feel nothing but her old fondness for her.

'I'm always going to look after you, Vety,' she heard her voice saying. 'I'm never going to let anyone hit you ever again.'

They sat by the river talking the afternoon away. Every little detail they remembered about the ghost coincided. It was exciting to begin with, but as the shadows began to lengthen and dusk began to fall, Weener's scalp began to prickle with fear and the rustling of the forest as it settled down for the night, seemed to be full of stealthy footsteps. She felt herself go cold and rigid.

'What's the matter?' Verity asked.

'I don't dare go home. Suppose he's there. Suppose he's waiting for us.'

Verity shuddered and went pale. 'We can't stay here.' she said tremulously.

Weener moved closer. 'Oh Vety, what are we going to do?'

Verity bit her lip. 'We could go along the river bank. It's much longer, but it wouldn't be so frightening, would it? Shall we do that then Weener?'

Weener nodded as they both stood up. Now she was

grateful for Verity's hand as they hurried along the bank. The trees seemed to be moving closer to the path, crowding them in.

'Mummy said we should never stay out in the dusk. She says it's the worst time for dirty men.'

Verity moved closer. 'Do you think Kurt's ghost is dirty, then?' she asked.

'I don't know,' Weener wailed. 'Oh Vety, why didn't we go home sooner?'

The shadowy path took them to the side of the little house which was set back from the river. The wall looked softly pink in the last light of the setting sun. Weener was about to smile at Verity when suddenly her relief turned to paralysing fear.

Kurt's ghost was lounging in the shadow of the wall. Verity must have seen it because she froze too and they both stood motionless while the ghost took one last puff of its cigarette, then threw it to the ground and disappeared around the back of the house.

'Did you see?' Weener asked against the constriction in her throat. Verity nodded. 'And you'll tell Mummy?' Weener asked urgently. Verity nodded again. Weener squeezed her hand gratefully and they walked in silence up to the house.

XV
The end of Friendship

As Weener had expected, Pauline was not allowed to come down for tea. Eva was surprisingly cheerful, but Weener felt she was putting it on and that she was secretly jealous of her for being so friendly with Verity. She kept catching Eva looking at them with a funny expression on her face.

'You had a good game, I think.' she said as her eyes accidentally met Weener's.

'Oh, we just walked and talked, you know.' Weener answered casually.

'So much to see in the forest,' Eva went on. 'Sometimes even, you may see the men who look after. You saw perhaps such a man?'

'No,' Verity said unguardedly. 'We only saw —'

Weener kicked her as she interrupted, 'Rabbits, birds — you know, things like that.'

Eva looked suspicious. 'And what did you see, *Liebling*?' she asked Verity.

'Oh, rabbits and birds — and Weener threw stones in the river and it made beautiful ripples. It was lovely, Eva. It's so kind of you to bring us here.'

Eva laughed. 'Perhaps tomorrow I will come too.'

Weener felt a stab of dislike for Verity even though her crawling had done the trick and averted Eva's suspicion.

'And now, for two good girls, I have a treat.' Eva dipped under the table and brought out two lollipops. 'One for each,' she laughed as she handed them over, 'to eat in bed, so now, I think you will be glad to go.'

They both thanked her and promised to go straight to sleep. But, of course, sleep was impossible. It gave such a lovely, tingling feeling of impending danger to talk about the ghost while being tucked up in bed, that Weener could not leave the subject alone. She was so relieved that Verity could see it too. As the night wore on, Verity's answers became drowsy and more mechanical, but Weener was determined not to let her sleep. 'I've got to go to the lav.,' she said at last.

'Mmm' Verity answered unsympathetically.

'Well, don't go to sleep,' Weener said importantly. 'The ghost might be in there.'

'Call me if you see anything.'

Weener looked at her doubtfully as she crawled out of bed. 'Open your eyes, or you might go to sleep by mistake.' Verity obeyed and Weener crept out of the room.

She had not really expected any trouble, but once she got on to the gallery, all her senses suddenly pricked to attention. Behind the landing window, a full moon was riding on a sea of ghostly clouds. Its lifeless light made strange, cold shadows around the door-frames and the bannisters. The little house was wrapped in a stillness which seemed loaded with impending danger.

She crept towards the bathroom and, as she reached it, she heard a shuffle, as if someone was standing on the other side of the door.

'Anyone in there?' she asked, and was frightened by her own thin voice. Nobody answered so she turned the handle. The door opened with a little creak and, as it did so, she was sure she heard footsteps crossing the bathroom floor. But when she looked, there was nobody there.

The lavatory seat was up and the pan was full of someone else's urine. Weener tutted to herself with annoyance as she flushed it and put the seat down, then she turned and began to pull up her nightgown.

She was facing the shower now and, as she looked absentmindedly at the shower curtains, a horrible realization came to her that there was someone standing behind them. It was not the same as when she had seen Pauline through the partition wall. The shadow on the white plastic folds was real and terrifyingly substantial. She let go of her half-hitched nightgown, sidled to the door and quietly slipped out on to the landing.

'Verity,' she hissed when she reached their room. 'Verity. Kurt's ghost. It's in the shower.'

Verity sat up, gazing straight in front of her with glazed eyes and then, amazingly, she rolled out of bed and walked determinedly to the door.

Weener followed her across the landing. 'Don't go in.' she whispered urgently, but Verity did not seem to hear her, and it was only when the bathroom door had closed in her face, that Weener realized Verity was still asleep.

Everything in Weener told her to follow Verity, but a deadening fear held her back. Instead she bent down and watched through the keyhole. She saw Verity walk across the little space of floor. She saw her pull back the curtains. She saw Kurt's ghost standing tall and terrifying in the shower and she heard the dull thud as he hit Verity over the head with the butt of the gun he was holding. Verity collapsed like a rag-doll and as she hit the floor, a little sigh escaped from her as if, at last, she had managed to do something really important. And in her heart, Weener knew her sister was dead. Half-crouching, she backed away from the door, then bolted for their room and threw herself into bed. She pulled the covers over her head and lay in a black paralysis of fear.

When Eva came in some minutes later, Weener pretended to be asleep. Eva's tread was heavy as she crossed the room and Weener, peeping round her bedclothes, saw that she was carrying Verity; rocking her with each step and crooning to her in German. Weener wanted to scream at her, 'Don't bring her in here. Don't make me sleep with a dead body.' But the greater fear of Eva finding out what she had seen, stopped her.

She watched Eva lay Verity's body tenderly on the bed and then go out of the room again. When she returned, she was carrying a little basin and a face flannel. She sat down beside Verity and, half-raising her, began to bathe her head. Weener watched for some moments and then asked involuntarily, 'Is she dead?' Eva started guiltily and turned around. 'What did you see, you wicked girl?'

Weener swallowed hard, knowing the danger she was in. 'I saw you carrying Verity in just now. Is she dead?'

'Of course she is not dead,' Eva reproved as she gently settled Verity back on the bed. 'She slipped in the bathroom and she has hit her head. She will be better tomorrow, you will see.' She kissed Verity, then stood up. 'Now go to sleep, you wicked girl.' she snapped as she left the room.

Alone in the dark, Weener hugged herself with excitement. 'You wait till I tell Mummy,' she whispered across to Verity, 'now she'll have to believe us, won't she? I expect she'll decide it's so dangerous here that she'll have to take us home.' But Verity did not answer and only her shallow erratic breathing gave any indication that she was still alive. Verity did not wake up the next morning. Eva put her into Weener's bed while she angrily stripped the covers and sheets from Verity's, as if they and they alone were responsible for her condition. The bed was made up with a completely fresh set and when it was finished and Verity had been decanted into it, it looked as if the covers had been painted on, or nailed into position.

Verity lay placidly on her back with the broad white sheet stretched symmetrically across her chest. There was not a flicker of expression on her face and the greenish-blue veins which seemed very clearly etched beneath the whiteness of her skin suddenly reminded Weener of the hands of a very old man she once had known. She shuddered and turned away.

'I should think she probably will die, wouldn't you, Eva?' she observed as she adjusted the drawstring on her new white socks.

'Of course she will not die, silly girl. Now go to the dining-room and eat your breakfast.'

Pauline was sitting at the table when Weener got downstairs. She looked up as if nothing had happened yesterday.

' 'Lo Weener.' she smiled.

Weener sat down and poured herself a cup of tea.

'No milk again.' Pauline said ruefully.

'Verity's ever so ill,' Weener remarked. 'I should think she's probably going to die.'

'Don't be so damn stupid,' Pauline snapped scornfully. 'Eva told me all about it. The stupid brat fell over in the shower. She'll be all right.'

Weener drank her tea in silence while she decided not to tell Pauline anything about what she had seen: it would be much better to save it all until their mother came home.

She spent that day loafing around the little house and sometimes trotting up to see how Verity was. But Verity did not wake up that afternoon or during the following night. She wetted the bed once, but Eva did not get angry with her. She simply and methodically remade the bed with fresh linen and Verity went on lying like a statue, her deathlike face hovering above the flawless sheet.

The next morning, the doctor arrived and, to Weener's immense relief, as his footsteps sounded on the bare wooden stairs, Verity frowned momentarily as though she had just remembered something, and then her eyelids opened. Weener shook her. 'Vety,' she hissed urgently, 'are you awake?'

Verity nodded.

'You've been asleep for a whole day and a night. The ghost hit you on the head in the shower. You will tell Mummy, won't you?' Verity opened her mouth, but before she could speak, Eva opened the door and ushered the doctor in.

'The poor little girl slipped in the shower this morning. She has been asleep now for two whole hours.'

'It's not true,' Weener started to say, but Eva pushed her out of the room and closed the door in her face.

Weener felt nothing but hatred for Eva as she went down

the stairs and her hatred made her so brave that she suddenly stopped midway and shouted at the top of her voice, 'Li-ar, li-ar, you're pants are on fi-re. Your nose is as long as a telephone wi-re!'

She went on shouting till Eva came out on to the landing. 'You wait until I tell Mummy!' she shouted up rebelliously. 'Just you wait, you German, you!' And then, seeing how menacing Eva looked, she turned and fled down the stairs, out of the house and into the shelter of the forest.

Eva came to the front door and Weener could have screamed with laughter to see her so furious, but she was clever enough to stay hidden and wait for her mother.

When, at last, the car drove up, Weener was ready. 'Mummy, Mummy, Mummy!' she screamed as she raced towards her.

Her mother stopped and had just enough time to turn before Weener launched herself and clasped her tightly around the waist. 'Weener! Darling!' she gasped.

'I've got to talk to you, Mummy,' Weener said with her face pressed close against her mother's arm.

'In a minute, darling. I must see Verity first.'

'It's about Verity. She didn't fall over in the shower. A ghost hit her on the head with a gun and, do you know what, Mummy?' she looked intently up at her mother and dropped her voice, 'I think it was Kurt's ghost.'

Her mother looked down at her with an expression Weener could not understand. 'Oh, Weener, Weener, in-betweener,' she asked at last, 'what am I going to do with you?'

Weener backed away a little. 'It's true, Mummy!' she shouted, 'and Eva's covering it up. She says Verity's been asleep for two hours — but she hasn't. She's been asleep for two whole nights and a day!'

Her mother paused, 'Are you sure?'

'Cross my heart and hope to die. It's true, Mummy. You must believe me.'

Suddenly they were hurrying forward, hand in hand.

113

'Come on,' her mother's voice was decided, 'we're going to get to the bottom of this.' She said no more as they marched upstairs and into the bedroom.

'Ah, Mrs Edwards,' the doctor smiled, but they walked straight past him.

'Verity, Verity darling,' her mother said as she sat down on the edge of the bed. 'What happened? Can you remember? Can you tell me, darling?'

Verity blinked as she looked past her mother to Eva and then she smiled the picture smile. Weener felt her heart sink. At last Verity shook her head. 'I don't remember.' she said innocently.

Weener pushed forward. 'Tell her about the ghost. You must, Vety. You must! You promised!'

Verity closed her eyes, but Weener got hold of her shoulders and shook her. 'Wake up!' she shouted imperiously. 'You promised you'd tell her. You promised!'

She felt Eva's hands on her shoulders and in a blind and desperate misery, she felt herself being propelled across the room. 'We'll have a talk, darling. I promise. Just as soon as I've spoken to the doctor.' her mother's voice was gentle, almost tender. But Weener, gazing through swimming tears, knew that her mother would never believe her. And as she left the room, an aching loneliness took hold of her because she knew she would never be able to forgive Verity's betrayal and that she would never trust or love her ever again.

XVI
Fritz

Because of Verity's concussion, they could not move to the
new posting with their father. He left on the Tuesday in a
flurry of male importance and then the rest of the family had
to hang around the Kaiserhof for a whole week, waiting for
Verity to get better.

It was annoying, but Pauline decided there was one con-
solation: hanging on that extra week meant they would be
going by road rather than rail. Their mother had ordered
two army lorries to be specially converted for them. Pauline
loved army vehicles: there was such a feeling of power and
excitement about them. She would have much preferred to
go by jeep: jeeps went so much faster, and, sitting up high in
the swaying back always made her feel important, as if she
really was part of the army of occupation. Still, you got the
same looks of envy and admiration in a lorry and, as her
mother had pointed out, jeeps were not really very comfortable. They had a long way to go. It was going to take
them at least two days, possibly three, if they hit any delays.

The converted lorries were completely amazing. Standing
in the early morning haze, Pauline was filled with admiration for her mother. The floors had been covered with
flock-filled mattresses and the first lorry, which they would
be travelling in, had four big armchairs riveted to the floor,
straight through the ticking covers. They looked like
thrones perched high in the air under a khaki awning. There
were piles of grey army blankets in case they felt cold, and a
great wicker hamper of food.

The second lorry was for the luggage. Their mother had
ordered a crate to be made to take their belongings, but

when it arrived, it turned out be a huge wooden box. It took three men to carry it downstairs and, as she watched it being lifted aboard, Pauline could not help smiling to herself.

Last night, when everybody was asleep, she had crept into the living-room and quietly unpacked Verity's picture. In her mind's eye, she could still see the vapid face of the fat little girl lying on the floor and she could still hear the delicious sound of breaking glass as she ground the heel of her shoe into it. Nobody else had heard anything: nobody else knew that the picture now lay broken in its wrapping.

'Oh heavens,' she said to her mother as the men heaved the box into the back of the lorry. 'I hope nothing gets smashed.' Her mother gave a rueful little shrug. 'Fingers crossed.' she said, which made Pauline laugh even harder inside herself.

Eva was travelling with the luggage and, as they were giving Fritz a lift as far as Hamburg, two chairs had been fixed into the second lorry for them. Pauline was pleased to notice that they were not nearly so big and important as the family chairs.

It was funny seeing Fritz out of his waiter's uniform. He seemed even smaller in his thin, shiny, blue suit, but there was an air of pent up excitement about him and he had a red carnation in his buttonhole which Pauline decided made him look very colourful. 'Can I go with Fritz?' she asked involuntarily. 'Please, Mummy, please? Because I might never see him again.'

He smiled at her and tweaked her pigtail. 'And what of your nanny, Fräulein Päulein?' he asked and then quite unexpectedly, he swung her into the back of the first lorry. His hands were surprisingly strong and the air around him was full of the heavy scent of his hair-cream. Pauline looked down at him with a new admiration. 'Perhaps after the first stop you can sit with us for a little and we can talk.' he smiled.

She nodded enthusiastically as he turned to her mother, 'Madame,' his voice was deep with reverence, 'madame,

116

allow me.' He clambered up into the back of the lorry and reached down to help her up. Once she was aboard, he ushered her into the far chair and spread a rug over her knees with the same little flourish he usually reserved for napkins. Pauline turned aside to hide a smile. She could see her mother did not really like his attentions but was frightened of hurting his feelings.

'And now for the little ones.' He was in total command of the situation and was obviously enjoying himself as he swung down and reached towards Weener.

'I don't want to go in the back,' she told him coldly as she pulled away. 'I'd better go with the driver or I might be sick.' Although she said the words to him, she was obviously speaking to her mother and he turned questioningly to her.

'Yes, all right.' Her mother's reply could have been to either of them.

With a shrug of indifference, Weener stomped away and climbed unaided into the passenger seat.

Fritz lifted Verity into the chair beside her mother, then pulled up the tail-flap and slammed the fasteners home.

The driver switched on the engine and the lorry suddenly growled and shook itself into life.

'See you at lunch.' Pauline called, and was pleased when Fritz turned to give her his special smile.

There was something tremendously majestic about the way they swung out of the Kaiserhof grounds. The half-waking windows looked down on them in surprise, as though they had never heard the heavy throb of lorries changing gear before that morning. The tall yellow building, with the sunlight dancing on its walls and roof, was already a thing of the past; slowly diminishing in importance as it receded into the distance. Pauline watched it until a bend in the road suddenly cut it off from view and then it was as if it had never been: as if they had never lived there.

Her mother seemed to feel it too because she suddenly stirred in her chair and called across to Weener. 'Are you all right there, darling?'

Weener half-turned but she did not smile. 'Yes thank you, Mummy.' she answered politely. The heavy vibration shook her voice a little, but she did not seem to notice or to care and after a few minutes, she turned back again to pin her attention on the road in front.

Her mother sighed and Pauline smiled at her. 'Don't worry, Mummy,' she said reassuringly, 'She can't go on sulking forever.'

Her mother turned to Verity, who was clinging to the arm of her chair, gazing out of the back of the lorry, her face tense with concentration. 'What are you doing, darling?' she asked.

'I'm counting the trees. Then we'll know how many there are.'

'Oh, don't be so stupid!' Pauline could not keep the scorn out of her voice. 'You can't count all the trees. What about the ones you can't see?'

'I'm counting the ones by the road,' Verity retorted with frosty dignity.

Pauline bit her lip. Throughout that week, Verity had been endlessly provoking. It was not so much her answering back that infuriated Pauline, it was her open air of knowing she was protected. It was amazing the fuss everybody had made over what, after all, had been diagnosed as mild concussion. All the grown-ups knew what the doctor had said and yet they gave in to her fake headaches and her going to bed to call attention to herself. Pauline knew she was being openly provoked, but she refused to be drawn. It would be time enough to take Verity in hand when they got to their new posting.

Lately, Pauline had begun to develop a surprising patience and an enormous amount of self-control. She was secretly very proud of the fact that she could now hold a rage within herself whilst seeming to be happy and loving to the outside world. She could hold on for days until the right moment presented itself to bring the rage to its fulfilment. It gave her a delicious sense of power knowing that nobody could understand what made her do the things she did. It was not her fault if the people around her were so stupid they could only comprehend the minute of time which was 'now'. Pauline had begun to think on a very broad spectrum and sometimes her understanding and cleverness amazed even her.

So now, she turned away from Verity who went on doggedly counting trees, and looked instead at the back of Weener's head. 'She is a funny old cove, isn't she.' she remarked. Her mother glanced at her, then shrugged. 'Oh, she'll come round. She was very upset by Verity's fall, you know.'

Pauline nodded. 'You know that time she went into a sulk when we were little: you know, during the war?'

Her mother considered it for some moments. 'Good heavens, yes,' she said at last. 'Fancy you remembering that.'

Pauline smiled briefly. It was just as well for her mother to know that she never forgot anything. 'Well, it was all because Aunty Dorothy gave her an orange. She told me about it when the sulk was over. She hates oranges, you see.' She was pleased to see that her mother looked perplexed and a little bit shocked.

'How extraordinary.' she murmured.

'Three hundred and eighty-two. Three hundred and eighty-three.' Verity said clearly, then lapsed into silence.

Pauline felt her lip curl in contempt, but she held her tongue and turned her attention to the road.

The most remarkable thing as they wound their way through the forest was the complete absence of any other traffic. The pine trees swayed gently from time to time as an overhanging branch caught the side of the lorry, but on the whole, everything was tranquil beneath the glittering blue sky. Even when they left the forest and started out along the broad main road, they found it to be completely empty.

Once, an army lorry on its way to the forest passed them in a flurry of dust. The soldiers in the back hung over the tail-board, hooting and cheering while Pauline waved to them. When they had gone, the road seemed to be doubly deserted.

They passed by miles of empty fields and then the road took them through a string of little towns. Here, it was narrow and sometimes the little cobbled streets only just allowed the lorries to pass. The noise of the engines echoing against the walls was deafening, but nobody looked up. All the people they passed had the same look of concentrated misery. Heads down, shoulders stooped, they hurried through the streets as if they had not even noticed it was a beautiful day or that anything as exciting as an army lorry had come to visit them.

Another strange thing Pauline noticed was that clumps of bright green grass were growing between the paving stones and along the kerbs. There was bomb damage everywhere. Sometimes a whole street of houses and shops would be missing: only a wall with a few ragged posters showed there had ever been life there. Pauline was used to seeing bomb-sites, but somehow they were different in England. Perhaps it was because they grew over so quickly with willow-herb and other wild flowers. Here, the rubble had been left exactly as it had fallen and the land, choked with plaster and masonry, seemed to be as defeated as its population.

The shops that were left standing were all heavily boarded with rough planks of wood. She wondered if there was anything for sale in them and, if not, she wondered where the people did their shopping. The only person she saw who might have been shopping was a little old woman carrying a loaf of bread inside her coat.

'Where did you get your bread?' Pauline called in German above the roar of the engine. The woman pulled her coat closer around the bread and shot Pauline a hard, glittering glare before she turned and hobbled quickly down a narrow side street.

'Don't shout at people, Pauline,' her mother said as she touched Pauline on the shoulder. 'It's very rude.'

'I only asked her where she got her bread from.' Pauline

answered indignantly. 'I mean, all the shops we've passed are closed. Where do they do their shopping?'

'I think it's all bought on the black market.'

Pauline nodded gravely and made up her mind to ask Fritz where the black market was: it sounded very exciting.

As soon as they had left the last town behind and were out among the empty fields again, their mother decided to stop for lunch. The lorries sounded weary as they ground to a halt, and even Pauline felt stiff as she jumped down. Weener joined them as they walked a little way into the cornfield, but she still refused to talk to anyone.

By the time they got back, Fritz had set up a folding table in their lorry and spread it with a delicious looking lunch. Their mother looked at it doubtfully.

'Oh Fritz,' she said coaxingly, 'wouldn't it be much nicer in the open?'

His eyes, as he looked back at her, were expressionless.

'Come on,' she added, 'the drivers will give you a hand.'

'Madame, for you I would gladly —' he stopped in embarrassment and then he quickly added, 'it is the little girls, madame. If we should need to leave quickly —'

She looked at him as if her mind was assimilating a coded message, then she nodded. 'You're right, of course.' she said with some embarrassment as she allowed him to help her up again.

Pauline could not help feeling her mother was stupid to give way so easily, particularly as she was right. It would have been much nicer to eat by the side of the road.

Fritz seemed to be aware that he had spoiled their treat and he made an extra special fuss of them as he served their meal. Pauline pondered on their reactions while she ate, until quite suddenly she remembered what Wolfgang had said and her mind threw up the answer.

'Good heavens,' she said, 'they wouldn't really kill us for our food, would they?'

Weener and Verity looked up simultaneously.

'Who?' Verity asked.

121

'The Germans, stupid,' Pauline said scornfully. 'And don't talk with your mouth full.'

'Pauline,' her mother snapped, 'don't speak to your sister like that.'

'Well, she shouldn't, you know.' Pauline kept her voice conciliatory because she badly wanted an answer to her question. 'But they wouldn't, would they, Mummy?' she went on. 'The Germans wouldn't really kill us for our food?'

Her mother looked uncomfortable. 'No, darling, of course they wouldn't.'

Pauline looked up at Fritz who hid his emotions behind a polite cough. 'If madame will excuse me, I will serve her coffee and then see if the nanny has eaten. It is better we should not stay too long.'

He cleared the dirty plates into a wicker basket then poured a cup of coffee from a thermos flask. He went about his work with a careful concentration, which showed that his holiday mood had completely evaporated.

Pauline watched him as he carried the wicker basket and the folding table round to the second lorry and then she looked at the drivers. Neither of them had moved since they had stopped. She concluded that anything they needed to do must have been done in the road while the family was in the cornfield. They must be afraid to leave the lorries, she decided, which must mean they really were in danger. She found the idea so exciting, she forgot to ask if she could change places with Eva and so she did not see Fritz again until they finally reached Hamburg that evening.

Hamburg turned out to be a terrible disappointment. There was nothing to show they were arriving in a town: nothing except for acres and acres of blackened rubble.

'My God,' her mother shuddered and lit a cigarette. 'Oh, my God, how awful.'

'What?' Pauline asked.

'This is Hamburg.'

Pauline looked around, wondering how she knew, and noticed an archway standing out, black and incongruous against the greying evening sky. It was the only thing left intact and its total uselessness seemed to mock the ruins around it.

The lorries ground on, bouncing occasionally as they crossed a set of tramlines. Sometimes they passed bundles of black cloth perched on ruined walls. In that fading light, it took Pauline some time to realize that they were old women who nodded as if agreeing with themselves that the devastation was total.

'Eva said that Hamburg was destroyed.' Verity said, more to herself than anybody else. 'It was the English who bombed it, you know: not Hitler.'

'Well, he did a pretty good job on Coventry.' their mother snapped, and then, seeing the second lorry was slowing down, she turned and called to the driver, 'Stop here, please.'

The second lorry eased forward, overtook them and then pulled up with its tail-board touching their nose. Fritz came hurrying around, carrying a battered cardboard suitcase.

'Oh Fritz, you can't stay here.' her voice seemed to be choking against tears.

He shrugged. 'It is my town. Somebody must rebuild it.'

She tossed her cigarette over the tail-board and was about to take his hand when, suddenly, a gang of wolfish children emerged from nowhere. Their stick-like bodies were tense beneath their threadbare clothes as they fought with desperate ferocity over the cigarette butt.

She passed her hand over her face. 'Oh God, how awful. How awful.' she breathed, then, seeming to collect herself, she reached into her handbag and brought out the packet of cigarettes.

Fritz acted instantaneously. With one hand he pushed the packet back into her handbag and with the other, he vaulted lightly over the tail-board of the lorry. '*Schnell!*' he shouted.

The driver put his hand on the horn to warn his friend and both engines roared back to life.

The children in the street stopped fighting. For a moment

123

they seemed to waver and then, as the lorries drew away, they began to run in a pack after them. With thin arms outstretched, they pleaded, '*Bitte, bitte! Gnädige Frau, bitte!*'

'Stop.' their mother screamed, but Fritz, holding tightly onto her handbag roared, 'Drive!' and it was Fritz the drivers chose to obey.

One of the children caught hold of the guy-rope on the canvas awning. He swung by his thin arm until Fritz beat him to the ground.

'Stop it.' Pauline heard her mother shout. 'You must let me help them.'

Fritz did not reply until they were clear of the pack, who melted back into the shadows like a nightmare. Then he said gently, 'If I had let you, madame, you would not have helped them. It would have led to murder.' He turned to the driver. 'Stop here.' he said briefly.

The lorry stopped suddenly and he jumped to the ground. 'Goodbye,' his voice was like an echo of the hideous town. 'Goodbye, dear madame.'

Pauline never saw him disappear. One minute he was standing by the lorry and the next minute he was gone, as though the monster of devastation had swallowed him alive.

Their mother closed down the canvas flaps and they sat in stunned silence until they reached their hotel. And by the time they got there, Fritz was as much a part of the past as the half-forgotten Kaiserhof.

XVII
The man with no face

Most of Weener's mind was asleep. The little bit that was still awake was only conscious of discomfort and the endless throbbing noise of the lorry engine. Her mouth was dry, her legs tingled and her head ached, so that every time sleep totally overtook her, that ragged little corner of her mind was roused and reminded her that she hated riding in lorries even if she did have the front seat.

The Shonkerdinkles were sitting in their garden. They made such a happy, golden picture, that Weener longed to join them, but every time she got near Lord Shonkerdinkle's deck-chair, the lorry hit a rut in the road or had to change gear and the picture faded.

She fidgeted in her seat and the driver, thinking she was awake, said something to her in German. She knew he must have leant quite near to speak to her because she felt his breath on her forehead, but though she liked him, she could not rouse herself enough even to understand what he had said.

She pushed her aching head against the back of the seat and sighed with relief. As if by magic, the noise of the engine died away and she was free to go into the garden.

Lady Shonkerdinkle was dusting the trees with her feather duster. She looked so fragile and pale that Weener immediately ran to her.

'Dear lady,' she said, 'pray let me carry that heavy duster for you.'

A faint smile of relief played on Lady Shonkerdinkle's face as she passed the duster over. 'Dear child,' she breathed, 'always so willing and dependable.'

To Weener's surprise, the duster was intolerably heavy that day and it made her arm ache horribly as she reached up to the nearest tree. As soon as she began to work, she found out the reason why. It was full of dust which suddenly exploded over her, knocking her sideways, before it trapped her in a suffocating mountain. Lord Shonkerdinkle rushed up to help her.

'Come on, chicken,' he said briskly as he flicked the duster against her face. 'Up you come.'

Weener felt immediately irritated. Lord Shonkerdinkle's remarks were usually so elegant. 'I should think, Lord Shonkerdinkle, you should let me get used to dusting your trees, if we really are going to be married,' she told him distantly.

There was a shout of laughter close to her ear. She opened her eyes unwillingly and looked straight into her father's face. 'My God!' he gasped as he lifted her out of the lorry. 'My God, you kids are worth a guinea a minute.'

Weener felt mortified. She could not imagine how she could have mistaken her father for her friend. She closed her eyes while she cursed herself for having spoken aloud.

'Pussy-cat,' she heard her father say after he had carried her for some moments. 'Pussy-cat, you'll never guess what this kitten of yours has gone and done.' He squeezed Weener closer and began to laugh again. Weener bit her lip with embarrassment and opened her eyes.

Her mother was standing by the gangway of a little white boat, her hand resting on the guide rope. 'Don't tease her, darling.' she murmured.

Weener began to struggle, but her father held her tight. 'Not teasing — telling you something you ought to know. She's got herself engaged. No, honestly she has — to a character by the name of Shonkerdinkle.' The last word came out with a shout of laughter. Weener hit his chest as hard as she could with her fist and, still shaking with laughter, he set her down on the ground. 'Only problem is,' he went on as she ran over to her mother, 'the fellow's a bit of a cad. Seems he won't let her dust his trees.'

Weener hid her face in her mother's coat, grateful for the protective arm that immediately encircled her.

'Were you having a dream, poppet?' It was such a casual and yet private remark that it somehow took all the sting out of Weener's shame. She looked up, vowing that if she ever had another sulk, it would not include her mother.

'Got a title, though,' her father went on as he joined them. 'Hurry along there, please, Lady Shonkerdinkle.' He gave Weener a little push towards the gangway and then added 'Ting-ting.'

'David, stop it,' her mother said wearily. 'They've been travelling for two days. They're exhausted.'

'Wooo.' He swept Weener up and carried her onto the boat. 'They'd better not be! Got a special party laid on for all of you tonight. You'll like that, won't you, me dear old chum?'

Pauline and Verity were already on the boat. Eva was standing between them in her cheap black coat and shabby felt hat. Weener turned away from her in disgust and took hold of her mother's hand as she came aboard.

'David,' her mother said. 'David, you'll have to cancel it.'

'Can't, Pussy-cat. Lots of very important people — all dying to meet you and the kids.' He bent down and kissed her. 'Don't worry, it's all laid on. You've only got to look beautiful.'

Weener looked from one to another. There was a current of feeling between them which disturbed her. She felt, suddenly, that her mother was vulnerable, so she held onto the little gloved hand and squeezed it reassuringly. The response was the complete opposite of what she had expected.

'Eva,' her mother's voice took on a distant, imperious note, 'take the children below. It's rather chilly for them out here.'

As Weener trooped after her sisters, she heard her father say, 'I just don't understand you. I mean, one minute you're

127

complaining because we don't spend enough time with the kids and then, when I lay something on that includes them — you go all hoity-toity.'

She sighed. 'I'm just tired.' Then, seeing that Weener was loitering, she added, 'Go on, Weener. I'll be down in a minute.'

A little flight of varnished steps took Weener down into the cabin. There were benches round the sides with tartan cushions on them. Verity was sitting with Eva, who had already brought out her knitting. From the look of it, she was making yet another white sock.

Pauline was kneeling on the bench opposite with her nose pressed to the window. Weener made her way over to her while the boat swayed uncertainly beneath her feet. She scrambled up and knelt as far away from Pauline as she could get.

'That's Nordseeheim,' Pauline remarked. 'It's quite nice, isn't it?' Weener shrugged dismissively although she found the port exciting. She could see the quay and its huge capstans, each with a thick rope coiled around it. The boat beside them was broad-bowed and painted navy-blue. Weener liked the way it lay in the water, gently rolling on the swell.

'This is a special boat,' Pauline went on. 'It's only ever used for important people.'

Weener looked round at her in surprise. She was not used to Pauline talking to her when she was in a sulk.

Pauline smiled. 'Nice to know we're important, isn't it?'

Weener nodded. 'I haven't half got a headache. I hope this boat isn't going to be as noisy as the lorries.'

'You have a headache?' Eva's voice was full of alarm. 'Then you must lie down, Fräulein.' She stood up but, as she did so, the boat lurched and the engine, which had been quietly whirring, suddenly roared to life. Eva was thrown back on the bench again as the boat pulled sharply away from the quay.

Pauline and Weener turned their backs on her, smiling as

they moved closer together. 'Hope we're going to enjoy living by the sea,' Pauline observed. 'Mummy says it's really smashing and there's lots of sand.'

'You went to the seaside once, didn't you?' Weener asked deferentially. 'When you were little, before the war.' Pauline nodded then sighed, 'But I'm afraid I don't remember it though. Gosh,' she added excitedly, 'we're out in the open sea!'

It was true. They had left the harbour behind and now the boat was whizzing through the ominous grey water. Weener suddenly remembered how she had been cheated on her last boat ride, so she turned to Eva and said distantly, 'I really do have a splitting headache and I think I'm very probably going to be sick. May we go on deck, please?'

Eva stood up. 'I will ask the mother,' she muttered as she made an uncertain path to the cabin door.

As soon as she was gone, Weener nudged Pauline. 'That should get us out of here. They only said we've got to stay below because they're having a row.'

'What a swiz!' Verity lisped from the other side of the cabin. Weener and Pauline looked at her distantly, then turned their backs.

'The father has given permission that you may leave the cabin,' Eva told them through the open door. 'You are to come with me, please.'

Weener smiled to herself with private amusement. Ever since they had got back from the little house in the forest, Eva had been formal and deferential; sometimes she had been almost as humble as when she first started to look after them. Although Weener knew that nobody believed her about Kurt's ghost, the fact that she had seen it and had sulked for a whole week about it, had made Eva just a little bit wary of her.

Now that they were on the open sea, the boat moved so erratically that it was impossible to walk in a straight line. As soon as she got on deck, Weener saw the reason why and was immediately frightened by it. The grey water was heaving with sullen waves and the little boat had to smack its way through them. It seemed very fragile to be pitted against such a vast and relentless opponent.

She made her way over to her mother and hung on to her hand. 'Have we got to go very far across the sea?' The wind whipped her voice away, throwing it out into the white spray the boat churned up behind them.

'That's where we're going.' Her mother pointed to a tiny island in the distance. 'It's very small, isn't it?'

Weener nodded. Like the boat, it seemed frighteningly defenceless against the cold North Sea, but as she watched, the speck of land grew bigger, until, quite suddenly, they were rushing towards a substantial shore, which finally developed into a walled harbour. The boat roared into the port, then swung majestically towards its anchorage.

Weener took a deep breath. One of the best things about coming out of a sulk, she decided, was that everything seemed so real and clearly drawn. She felt a mounting tide of elation. The harbour was wonderful; loud with the noise of lapping water and boats grinding against their moorings. Seagulls screamed as they endlessly wheeled and swooped through a forest of white masts; their sleek bodies almost luminous against the dull grey sky. 'What a smashing place.' she breathed involuntarily as she watched the gangway being lowered.

'Think you might like living by the sea, chicken?' her father teased.

Weener was too excited to remember any grudges. 'Oh yes,' she beamed up at him. 'Thank you, Daddy. It's really, really smashing.' He laughed and suddenly she was flying up into the air among the seagulls. 'That's my girl,' he shouted, then lowered her so that she was level with his chest. 'We're going to have such fun,' he went on as he cuddled her to him. 'We're all going to do things together.'

Weener giggled and kissed his cheek. 'Really?'

He nodded, then turned to shoot a triumphant look at her

mother. 'Boss's orders. Says we haven't been seeing enough of one another. So, it's all got to change, you see.'

A part of Weener's mind told her she was being used to annoy her mother, but she was so happy that she pushed the suggestion aside and twined her arms around his neck while he carried her down the swaying gangway.

'Think you'd like to go to a real grown-up party?' he asked as he put her down and then began to walk with her along the jetty.

'Oh yes, please Daddy!' she shouted. 'Oh gosh, it's the one thing I've always wanted to do. Are there going to be cocktails? Are there, Daddy?'

He stopped and turned back. Her mother was a little way behind with Pauline and Verity on either side of her.

'Well, I've got one customer for my party,' he called to her. 'Pity the other two won't be coming.'

Pauline looked up at her mother disbelievingly. Verity's lower lip pushed forward and began to quiver.

Her father laughed and hurried on again. 'Come on, my lovely,' he said to Weener, 'got to get you all prinked up and beautiful.' Weener held her breath. She had never felt so special and important before.

He lifted her into the back of a jeep which was waiting beside the jetty, then climbed up and sat down close beside her. 'Come on, you slowcoaches,' he shouted. 'Me and my girlfriend want to go to a party.'

'What party?' Pauline asked as she climbed aboard and took the seat opposite them.

He half-stood up and reached out a hand to help their mother, but she ignored it.

'Come on, darling,' she said wearily as she lifted Verity a little way off the ground. 'You know you can do it if you want to.' Verity blinked, then seemed to collect herself and scrambled into the back of the jeep. Still ignoring the offered hand, her mother pulled herself up and settled down between Pauline and Verity.

'I wish I knew what party it was that Vety and I won't

131

be going to.' Pauline glanced briefly at her father, then shrugged as if the remark was supposed to be rhetorical.

In front of them, the driver turned on the ignition and began to rev up the engine.

'Oh, it was just a little something I laid on,' her father answered casually. 'Thought you might enjoy it. Dreadfully disappointed to hear that you're too tired to come.'

Pauline looked at him indignantly. 'I'm not!' she said hotly, 'I mean, I'm the eldest. I can understand about Verity. She's much too young anyway. But I'm the eldest!'

Verity's lower lip trembled again and a fat tear slid down her cheek. 'I'm not too young,' she sobbed. 'I'm not young at all and I'm not tired either.'

Weener bit her lip, but her father slid an arm around her and she immediately felt more special than guilty.

'Oh dear,' he said, smiling conspiratorially at her, 'seems we've really set the cat among the pigeons.'

The jeep began to pull away and head towards a sandy road. 'Stop!' Verity shrieked. 'We've forgotten Eva!'

'Don't be silly, darling,' her mother patted her shoulder. 'She's following on with the luggage.'

Pauline smiled grimly. 'Yes, and I suppose she'll be going to the party, while we have to go to bed.'

'Don't be silly, Pauline. Of course she won't be going.' her mother snapped.

'Well, I don't see why Weener can go and we can't. It just seems so unfair.'

'Put that way,' her father mused, 'it does sound a bit of a mouldy deal, doesn't it? What do you think, me old chum?' he squeezed Weener's shoulder. 'Now, just suppose you were in charge, what would you do?'

Weener screwed up her eyes. Now she was sure she was being used to annoy her mother and, although she enjoyed being the favourite, she began to wish her father would stop making such a special thing of her.

'I think,' she began, but her mother quickly interrupted her.

132

'For God's sake,' she snapped, 'you're putting the child in an appalling position.'

'Can we go, then?' Pauline asked quickly.

'Oh, very well. I really don't see why you should want to go, but as your father insists —' Her voice was distant and Weener, feeling suddenly wretched, turned away to pin her attention on the road.

There was sand everywhere: fine puffs of sand which swirled in eddies on the low wind which swept across the island. And mixing with the sand were wisps and balls of ethereal white down which spiralled and danced, or bowled along the road at an unbelievable speed. Weener was entranced by it and put out her hand to try to catch some. But, just as a wisp came within her reach, her father grabbed her wrist and pulled her hand out of the way. 'It's spun glass,' he told her. 'You'll find it all over the island and you mustn't touch it, or you'll cut your hands to ribbons.'

Beyond the road, the land was humpy with tufts of coarse grass. Dotted around each hillock, huge brown sheep lay, munching slowly as they watched the jeep drive by.

It was not far to go before the jeep reached the *Offizier-heim*, which turned out to be a tall, holiday building with gleaming windows and sand-coloured walls. As soon as Weener ran into the entrance lobby, she knew she would be happy there: it was so light and full of the feeling of people enjoying themselves.

Their quarters were on the first floor and before she was even halfway up the stairs, Weener heard the murmur of voices, sometimes topped by a shout of laughter.

She was excited by the idea that she would soon be in the party enjoying herself like a real grown-up, but more than anything, she was thrilled with herself because, at last, she had learned the secret of how to make people love her. For the rest of my life, she thought as she ran up the broad marble stairs, I'll make myself be happy and full of fun and everybody will have to laugh and love me, just like Daddy does. The recipe was so simple that she was surprised she had never thought of it before.

She reached the landing first. The bannister rail was mahogany with wrought-iron supports. Weener clung to it and jumped up and down. Her head had begun to throb and hurt, but somehow the pain was in a separate compartment from the excitement and it did not bother her.

'Come on, you slowcoaches,' she shouted down to her family. 'There's a smashing party going on up here.'

Her mother hurried forward. 'Now calm down, darling,' she said as she reached the landing. 'You're much too excited.'

'No, I'm not!' Weener shouted. 'I'm just happy. I'm so happy I could do a somersault.'

Her mother brushed the back of her hand against Weener's cheek. 'Just take some deep breaths, or you know what'll happen — it'll all end in tears.'

The door in front of them opened and the noise and the smell of the party made Weener reel backwards. A white-coated waiter came forward as they crowded into the hall. 'Madame,' he said obsequiously, taking her mother's coat.

Weener's hands fumbled as she quickly peeled her own coat off and bundled it into the waiter's arms, then she ran through the open doorway into the party.

The room was on the corner of the building and the two outside walls were made entirely of glass which was surrounded by a balcony. It made the crowd of grown-ups look as if they were spilling out into open space. For a moment, Weener hesitated on the threshold until she suddenly spotted a face she knew. 'Uncle Denis!' she shouted as she hurled herself at him. 'Uncle Denis! Uncle Denis!'

His small, dark eyes glinted wickedly as he swept her up in his arms. 'What's my name? You've not got it quite right, my lovely.'

'You're Uncle Denis who's a menace!'

'Absolutely correct. Top marks to you, my girl. Now, where are your siblings?'

Weener did not understand the question so she asked,

'Are you going to give us a drawing lesson?'

He laughed. 'Not at the moment. Got a friend I'd like you to meet.' He turned to the woman who was standing beside him. 'Midge, like you to meet someone. This is a girlfriend of mine, but for the life of me, I can't remember which one.'

'How nice,' the voice was coldly distant.

Weener felt slightly crushed, but she was not going to let this Midge person spoil her beautiful mood. 'I'm Weener.' she told her, drawing out the syllables of her name so that it sounded like a lion's roar.

'How extraordinary.' Midge surveyed her with dislike. 'Tell me, Weener, aren't you a little old to play the baby?'

Weener felt a lump rise in the back of her throat which seemed to join up with the throbbing compartment in her head. She had not expected anybody to be nasty to her.

'Would you put me down, please Uncle Denis?' she asked politely. He obeyed with a rueful shrug which did nothing to make up for Weener's hurt.

'I'm sorry,' she heard Midge say. 'But, you know, I really can't stand children when they go brattish. I swear if I ever have any, they'll be brought up to be sensible and sincere.'

Uncle Denis squeezed Weener's shoulder, but she shrugged him off and moved away. Suddenly the people in the room seemed very tall and unapproachable. She could not see any of the family, which made her feel isolated and unwanted until a hand closed on her shoulder and a man's voice she did not recognise said, 'Don't look up.'

'Why not?' Weener asked.

'Because you'll be frightened.' The hand began to steer her through the crowd towards the balcony. 'You mustn't mind Midge,' the voice went on. 'She's had a pretty rotten time and it's rather soured her off.'

'Oh.' Weener tried to sound as if she understood. They were on the edge of the party now and she could see out across the balcony to where the sea pounded at the beach. She turned to look up at the voice and then, involuntarily, drew away.

135

The man, whose hand was still on her shoulder, was repulsively and horrifyingly ugly. From the eyebrows down, his face was a deep strawberry colour and pitted with dark holes. On one side, his jaw-bone seemed to be missing, and the skin hung so loosely around it that it almost seemed to be tucked into his shirt collar. His nose was a flattened disfiguration with flaring white nostrils.

Weener felt tears springing in her eyes and, against her will she began to sob.

'No,' he said, 'don't cry. I shouldn't have tried to help, but you seemed to be so unhappy.' He sat down in a wicker chair with his back to her. 'There,' he said. 'Now, if you like, you can stay and talk to me, but you won't have to look.'

She moved closer and pushed her fingers through the wicker-work so that she could feel his jacket.

'Sorry you were frightened,' he went on after a pause, 'but, you know, you shouldn't be. Let me ask you a question. Would you be frightened of a bombed house?'

Weener shook her head and, as if he had heard the gesture, he answered, 'Of course you wouldn't. It's just a building with its walls blown down. That's what happened to me, you see. A few of my walls got blown down, but that doesn't make me frightening — just a bit sad, like an old bombed-out house.'

In spite of herself, Weener found she was moving round to the front of his chair. 'You're very nice,' she told him, and his face crooked itself into a hideous smile.

'And so are you, poppet?' he answered. 'So what shall we talk about, hey?'

Weener climbed onto his knee. 'Do you think I'm brattish?'

'I think you're over-tired and a bit excited. You've come a long way, I believe.'

Weener nodded. 'Mmm, in army lorries.'

'Which, in itself, is enough excitement for anyone.' He took a sip from his glass.'

The remark was so calm and natural that it should have

136

relaxed her, but instead, she felt a mounting tension, coupled with a terror, that they would somehow be parted. Feeling unbearably sad, she looked away from him, across the balcony and down on to the beach.

There was somebody standing by the breakwater. He was too far away for her to be able to distinguish his features, but something about the slope of his shoulders and the way he smoked his cigarette made her know in her heart that it was Kurt's ghost. She felt herself go rigid.

'Cuddle me,' she said urgently to the man with no face. 'Please, please, cuddle me.'

He put an arm awkwardly around her. 'What on earth's the matter?'

Weener's teeth began to chatter. 'There's a ghost. Down there on the sand — there's a ghost. I thought we'd left him behind but he follows us everywhere.'

As if in answer to the statement, there was a loud crash from behind them and Weener screamed and clung to the man as he half-stood up.

'It's all right, poppet,' he soothed. 'Seems one of your sisters has fallen asleep on the drinks trolley. Come on, better see if we can help.'

Weener buried her face in his shoulder as he carried her across the room. When he stopped, she looked up and saw Verity, who had already been rescued from the trolley and was now asleep in her father's arms.

'Did the ghost hit her?' she asked, then screwed up her eyes because she knew it was the wrong thing to have said. Everything seemed to be getting very confused in her mind. The past and the present; the Shonkerdinkles and the ghost kept circling the throbbing in her head. She clung to the reality of the man with no face as she watched Eva come into the room and take Verity out of her father's arms.

'Time for bed, I think,' Eva observed a little drily.

'And that goes for you too.' her father turned and fixed Weener with a steely eye.

'No!' she screamed, fastening her grip around the

137

shattered neck. 'Please, Daddy, please don't make me leave him. I love him. He's my only friend in the whole world.'

The man with no face bent down, lowering her until her feet were touching the ground. But something had happened to Weener which had made her into a different person. Instead of letting go politely, she clung to him and sobbed against his shoulder, 'Please, please don't leave me. I'm frightened. There's a ghost outside.'

' 'Fraid you've picked the flirt of the family,' she heard her father say. 'Come on, Lady Shonkerdinkle,' he added as he began to pull her away, 'time for bed.'

The last shred of Weener's self-control snapped. She stepped aside from her friend and when she turned to face her father, she saw him as if through a red curtain and she felt only rage.

'I hate you.' Her voice was a whisper of her real feeling and she backed away while she gathered herself and her hatred to say something that would really hurt. 'You don't care for any of us. You only ever take any notice if you can get something out of it. I hate you! I hate you! You *Schweinhund*!' She roared the last word with the full volume of her lungs. It fell like a boulder on the suddenly silent room and, all at once, she was being propelled past the gaping adults. Only when they were out in the hall, did her father let go his vice-like grip on her arm.

'Never,' he said as he smacked her hard across the bottom, 'never, never let me hear you use that word again.'

Weener felt cold and dizzy. She did not understand what had happened, only that she had committed an unforgivable sin. She covered her face with her hands and began to sob convulsively.

'Eva.' There was an icy note to her father's voice. 'Oh, there you are. Now, this is a warning for you. If I ever hear one of my daughters swearing in your filthy language again, I won't only sack you, I'll see you never work again.' He turned on his heel and marched back to his party, while Eva led Weener sobbing to her new bedroom.

XVIII
School

After the way Weener and Verity had behaved at the party, Pauline was not surprised that her father stopped wanting the family to do things together. Their mother still made efforts to interest and amuse the children, but the family had drifted apart: Weener to her own separate world; Verity to a total dependency on Eva, and Pauline, who was growing up, really did not need anybody around her now.

After that ill-fated party, there were perpetual and stormy rows in the adult quarters. Pauline knew, because she had found a very good listening post. The new nursery had obviously once been one of the main rooms of the flat. It was big and sunny with a view over the sea. Originally, it had been connected to the drawing-room by a short corridor, but this had now been converted into a linen-cupboard. The door to the drawing-room could still be seen from inside the cupboard although it was papered over on the other side. Pauline now had her own small bedroom leading off the nursery, which had a doorway into the linen-cupboard too. This meant that for the first time in her life, she could really keep abreast with what was going on.

Their father wanted them to go to school, but their mother bitterly opposed him because there were no English schools on the island, so it would mean they would have to be put into a boarding-school. Verity was certainly too young and it would be such a shame to split them up, her mother reasoned, when they were all such good friends.

Pauline had discovered there was a law which said all children had to go to school. Her father never stopped quoting it; in fact, it came into every row, and her mother's only defence against it was to state coldly and flatly, 'I am not going to have my children regimented and bullied.'

The row would swing backwards and forwards, feeding on itself and gaining momentum. In Pauline's analysis, her father was vulnerable because he had girlfriends all over the place and was making such a fool of himself, he would eventually wreck his career. Her mother was vulnerable over the school issue. When either of them touched on the other's particular weakness, they would begin to shout and, from the occasional thuds and crashes, Pauline guessed they threw things at one another.

She found it very exciting listening at the cupboard door and, of course, she was intensely interested in how the school issue would be resolved. She did not tell Weener and Verity what was in the wind because neither of them could keep their mouths shut, and she wanted her parents to come to their conclusions without any outside influence. It would show which of them was the stronger, which, she was sure, would be a useful thing to know.

In the end, it was her mother who won by pulling a master stroke. She arranged for them all to go to the local German school which, in Pauline's opinion, was an ace decision. The school only opened in the mornings and, as all the lessons would be in German, nobody could expect her to do very well or get high marks. Another bonus was that, as everybody at the school would be German, they would all be her inferiors, so there would be no punishments and no trouble from older children or teachers.

Weener and Verity were shy and apprehensive on that first morning when Eva delivered them to the school-house. It irritated Pauline that they were so stupid they could not appreciate something that was so obviously to their advantage. For her part, she found that the school entirely lived up to her expectations.

They got there a little on the late side because they had to wait while Weener was sick, but they did not get into trouble about it.

As soon as they arrived in the classroom, Herr Greubel, the dusty, cadaverous schoolmaster, clicked his heels together and made a small speech about how grateful he was to their mother for choosing to honour his school with three such charming young ladies. Then, at a given signal, the children rose from their benches and chorused, 'Guten morgen Fräulein Pauline. Guten morgen Fräulein Doreen. Guten morgen Fräulein Verity.' The boys bowed and the girls curtsied while Weener and Verity gazed back in openmouthed astonishment. Pauline thanked Herr Greubel briefly and wished him good morning, which sent him into an ecstasy over her exquisite manners.

The school was divided into groups rather than classes, and Herr Greubel taught each group separately in the same room. Each little block of benches was allowed half an hour of his time while the rest worked on set exercises. Herr Greubel was painstakingly kind and patient and explained things so well, that Pauline found no difficulty in keeping up, even though she had been put in the senior section.

It was the easiest, most relaxed school she had ever been to. Every child had a little blackboard with a damp sponge attached. At the end of the morning, Herr Greubel checked the results of the set exercises and logged the marks he had given in a huge black book while the children sat with their hands on their heads. When all the marks had been given, the slates were wiped clean and everybody sang a song while Herr Greubel conducted with a chalky blackboard pointer.

Pauline had hoped that some of the children might talk to her when school was over. She followed them out into the sunny playground, but they all kept well clear of her.

'What do we do now?' Weener asked as she came up with Verity trailing behind her.

Pauline shrugged and looked around. The other children had formed a group around the gate. 'Join the queue, I suppose,' she muttered.

The children eyed them with cold suspicion and jostled closer to crowd them out.

'What are we waiting for?' Pauline asked the boy who was standing in front of her. He turned briefly without smiling. With his spiky hair-cut and broad, flat face, he looked exactly like a turnip as he stared at her, then, hunching his thin shoulders under his satchel straps, he turned away to gaze intently up the sandy road. Pauline felt she was being challenged. There was no excuse for such impertinence, particularly as she had spoken to him in German, so she punched his arm. 'Don't turn your back on me, turnip head,' she shouted into his protruding red ear. 'I asked you a civil question. What are we waiting for?'

He turned round, scratching his chin while he surveyed her thoughtfully. 'We wait for food, Fräulein,' he answered at last. Then, standing back, he put his hands on his hips and wiggled his ears at her as if it were the easiest thing in the world to do.

Pauline gazed at him in admiration. 'Gosh, I wish I could do that,' she breathed in English. 'How do you do it?' she demanded, remembering just in time to put the question into German. He shrugged.

'What's your name?' she asked.

'Gunther,' he answered simply, but the word was almost drowned by a cheer that went up from the other children and the noise of an army lorry that was heading down the road towards them.

The lorry drew up by the school gate and the children pressed towards it, laughing and chattering and clanking the billycans which suddenly each of them was holding. Two soldiers rolled back the canvas flaps to reveal a huge, steaming urn and a basket full of black bread.

The three girls hung back while the soldiers ladled a lumpy, yellow stew out of the urn into the waiting billycans. When everybody had been served, the soldier turned to Pauline. '*Essen?*' he asked with a thick English accent.

'I'm afraid we haven't got any billycans,' Pauline answered politely.

He dropped the ladle back into the urn. 'Crikey,' his voice

142

was loaded with shocked disbelief, 'are you English?'

Pauline nodded. 'And so are they,' she indicated Weener and Verity with a wave of her hand. 'They're my sisters and they haven't got billycans either.'

'Well push off home, then,' the soldier told her brusquely. 'Hanging about where you're not wanted. This 'ere's for German kids. I asks yer,' he went on rhetorically, 'now I've got me quantities wrong. 'Ere Fritz,' he shouted to a skinny, undersized child, 'bit more *Essen* for yer.'

Pauline watched with regret as her helping was shared among the other children. Eva had been getting very mean with the food lately and she really was quite hungry.

'Don't look at me like that,' the soldier scolded. 'You've got food at home. Now clear off!'

Pauline shrugged and led her sisters away from the school gate. 'We'll just have to ask Eva for something, I suppose. Bet she'll think of some excuse not to give us any.'

The prediction turned out to be right. After they had wandered back across the sand-dunes and played for a while on the beach outside the *Offiziersheim*, Pauline decided they really must have something to eat.

'We're very hungry,' she told Eva as they crowded into the nursery. 'What's for lunch?'

'Lunch?' Eva asked indignantly. 'You come in here at three o'clock and you ask what is for lunch? You have eaten at school. You are not hungry.'

'We didn't. The soldier wouldn't let us have any.' Pauline protested.

Eva laughed grimly. 'That I do not believe. Go away and play in the sunshine.'

As they wandered back down the stairs, Verity suddenly stopped and clapped her hand over her forehead.

'What's the matter?' Pauline asked.

'We forgot to go back to school.' Verity's voice was frantic and her face was a mask of anxiety.

Pauline surveyed her coolly. 'Do you like school, then?' Verity shook her head vigorously.

'Well, I vote we never go to school in the afternoons, then.'

'We'll get into terrible trouble.'

Pauline laughed aloud at her private joke. After all, it was not her fault if Verity was so stupid that she had already forgotten it was only a morning school. 'Come on,' she said, 'you can count the minutes while we play. We don't want to miss out on tea-time too.'

XIX
The hangar

So long as the term lasted, Pauline enjoyed living on the island. She made friends with the local children, so she was not dependent on her sisters for company any more. She was also learning to ride and she had discovered that she really loved horses. Her favourite was a chestnut mare called Rapuntzel. She had a wicked temper and had often thrown Pauline, but she galloped so beautifully across the sand, that Pauline always forgave her.

It was a pretty idyllic existence, but it all came to an end as soon as the holidays started.

The first blow was a crew of motley English children who arrived from their various boarding-schools. Pauline found them totally contemptible and yet her father insisted on her being polite to them. It was an order she found impossible to obey.

Pauline and her friends liked to play exciting games which were really trials of strength and nerve. Sometimes they would make a bonfire on the beach, then take it in turns to jump over while the fire was fed to make it bigger and bigger. The first person to baulk at the jump was the loser and Pauline had never lost yet.

The English children insisted on playing organized games with strict rules, and there were endless disciplinary arguments which made everything so boring. The boys were bossy and superior, while the girls were submissive and cliquey. They were frightened too of mines, which in Pauline's opinion was completely idiotic.

The island was smothered with mines: big rusty balls with ratchety nuts sticking out of them. So long as you did not tread on them or throw stones at them, they were perfectly safe. In fact, once, when the family went out for a walk with some friends, one of their many uncles had got over-excited and thrown Weener down a sand-dune into a whole nest of mines. She missed every one of them so nobody got hurt.

But the English children said they were dangerous and whined and carped about them so much that the army decided to blow all the mines up. This put whole areas of the island out of bounds, which meant the English children were confined to the beach behind the *Offiziersheim*.

Pauline hated it and she hated the endless boom from the exploding mines. She began to wonder whether there would be anything left of the island by the time the army had finished with it.

The second blow was a series of treats her mother laid on. As the island was a leave centre, she explained, it was important that everybody should enjoy themselves. Each afternoon was accounted for with a coach trip or a party.

To begin with, Pauline quite enjoyed the parties because the chefs were so clever at making exotic cakes and fancies. Sometimes there would be a whole dish full of meringue swans with their backs filled with cream, or a great cake with such a light and sumptuous centre, it had to be held together with cornflakes and sugar-roses. But after a few weeks, she began to tire of opulent living and to really long for a plain sardine sandwich and a good hunk of English fruit cake.

She felt restricted, and the fact that it was not being done with hardship or discipline, made the restriction trivial and irritating. She had not suffered a single rage since they had come to the island, but now she often felt that extraordinary change in her circulation which was the inevitable prelude to her getting into real trouble.

Eva was jittery too that summer. Pauline was sure she was up to something because she had such a knowing, yet guilty air about her. She went out on her own each morning and evening carrying an old canvas shopping bag. Pauline never

146

got a chance to look inside but she was convinced the shopping bag had food in it. She supposed it did not really matter if Eva gave food to some of the island people: they were all very poor and a lot of them went hungry. What she really objected to was the lack of discipline it led to in the nursery and when, one day, she came in and found Verity still in her pyjamas at eleven o'clock in the morning, she decided it was time somebody took the matter in hand. She reported what was happening to her mother who promised to have a word with Eva.

After that, Eva took Verity with her and Verity, who seemed to be getting progressively more stupid, would only give vague answers about what was going on.

Pauline had known, of course, that Eva would take reprisals for being sneaked against, but she had never imagined that her revenge would be so bizarre. Eva waited her time, getting progressively more jittery. Pauline watched and kept herself ready. She did not want Eva to strike when she was unprepared.

But no amount of preparation could have helped Pauline to cope with what eventually happened. One night when she was peacefully and innocently asleep, Eva came into her room and snapped on the electric light.

'Up.' she commanded briefly.

Pauline pulled the covers over her head and pretended not to hear, but Eva marched over and stripped the bed.

'You heard, you lazy girl. I said, "up".'

Pauline felt shocked and vulnerable lying on the bare bed. 'But it's the middle of the night.' she reasoned.

Eva grabbed her by the arm. 'When I give an order, you obey. I said to get up immediately!' She pulled Pauline roughly out of bed and Pauline, who had already learned to her cost that Eva was too strong for her, had to obey. Eva bundled her clothes into her arms. 'Now, get dressed,' she snapped. 'I shall be back in five minutes. If you are not dressed it will be worse for you.' She walked briskly over to the door.

'I'll tell my mother about this.' The distance between them made Pauline feel much braver.

Eva turned back in the doorway and laughed grimly. 'I don't think that you will, Fräulein. I don't think so.' Then she turned away and left the room, quietly closing the door behind her.

The tone of Eva's voice made Pauline realize she was in a trap. She wondered about hiding, but decided against it. Eva would be sure to find her and that would be humiliating. It was better to face it out, so she got dressed and ran quickly to the nursery.

To her relief, Weener and Verity were there, fully dressed and waiting for her. They both looked pale and half-asleep.

'What's going on?' she asked them.

'No talking. Put on your coat, please, Miss Pauline. It will be cold.' Eva's voice was more friendly now and when she passed the coat, her movements were not so abrupt.

Pauline looked questioningly at Weener who shrugged and pulled a face.

Eva put her finger to her lips. 'This is so exciting,' she told them as she took Verity's hand. 'Now, all quiet like little mice. My word, what a jolly prank this is!'

She opened the nursery door and surreptitiously checked the passageway outside. Against her will, Pauline found she was holding her breath.

Eva beckoned to them and they slipped out, one by one, behind her. The passageway was dark, which in itself was strange. Usually, a light burned there all night. Pauline wondered for a moment if her parents were away, but then she saw a band of yellow light spilling out from under the drawing-room door and heard the murmur of voices. She had a sudden impulse to run and tell her mother what was happening. Although Eva's mood seemed to have changed, Pauline did not trust her an inch and she was sure that something very nasty was about to happen.

Eva saw her waver and quickly pushed Weener and Verity

148

towards the service entrance. Then she hurried back and put a hand on Pauline's shoulder.

'It is a good treat,' she whispered. 'If this is not the best treat of your life, then you can say to me tomrorow, "Eva Königsberg, you are the biggest fool in all of Germany".'

Pauline opened her mouth to speak, but Eva put her finger to her lips and began to move silently down the passageway. Pauline followed; reluctantly at first, but then with a mounting excitement. Perhaps Eva was not so bad after all, she decided, as they tiptoed down the service stairs.

Once they were out of the building, Pauline realized how late it was. The navy-blue sky was freckled with stars and a broad-faced moon hung above the sea, making a path of silver ripples from the horizon to the beach.

Eva took Verity's hand and hurried them to the shelter of the sand-dunes.

'Where are we going?' Pauline asked excitedly.

'We go where you have so many times begged to be taken. Now, hurry, hurry, we do not want to waste a moment of our treat.' She looked down at Verity. 'This is so exciting, yes?'

As soon as they were clear of the *Offiziersheim*, Eva took them down onto the flatter sand. It was very ghostly to be by the sea at night. Everything was distorted and in some way threatening. A blackened piece of driftwood, sticking out of the sand, looked like a dead man's hand reaching up to clutch their ankles. The puffs of spun glass which by day delighted her, had suddenly become witches' hair and a thousand eyes seemed to glint wickedly from the dunes.

Weener suddenly stood stock-still and screamed shrilly. Eva grabbed her by the shoulder, but Weener shook her off and began to run forward across the sand. Pauline followed her.

A soldier was lying on his back; his face deathly white in the moonlight. Weener stopped beside him and gazed down. 'He's dead,' she breathed. 'What are we going to do?'

The soldier's chest was unnaturally humped as though he

149

had taken a deep breath and then forgotten to let it go.

'Perhaps he's been drowned,' Pauline whispered. 'We could give him artificial respiration.'

'He is drunk,' Eva said as she and Verity joined them. 'Quickly, you must come away.'

The soldier moved very slightly, then sighed deeply. 'I love you. I love you. I love you,' he murmured.

Eva smiled down at Weener. 'See,' she whispered as she led them gingerly round the prone body. 'You must never go near a soldier when he's drunk. It is very dangerous for little girls,' she told them after they had walked in silence for a little while.

'Why?' Pauline asked, but Eva did not bother to reply.

'Here we are.' she said with the air of a magician pulling a rabbit out of a hat.

Pauline looked around in astonishment. There was nothing special about the place. In fact, it was the most boring part of the island, because it was here that the beach stopped and gave way to a huge concrete platform which supported a derelict aircraft hangar.

'Come on,' Eva said breathlessly as she ran towards the hangar. 'My word, this is such a good treat!'

She led them round to the seaward side where there was a partially covered stairway climbing up the scaffolding leg. 'Come on, Miss Pauline, you go first and then Miss Doreen, you go after.'

Pauline turned and stared at her incredulously. 'We can't climb that. It's much too dangerous.'

Eva laughed scornfully. 'All this time you beg and you plead, "Let me climb the hangar, Eva." But, when I, with danger to myself, give you the chance, it turns out you are just a cowardy-custard.'

Pauline glared at her indignantly. 'Oh no I'm not,' she said and, flipping her plaits briskly across her shoulders, she began to climb.

After the first few steps, her fear left her. 'Come on, Weener,' she called. 'This is smashing.'

150

'Don't look down,' Eva shouted. 'Miss Doreen is behind you. Nobody is to look down, please.'

Pauline went on climbing, looking out of the cracked and broken windows beside her. The moonlight filtered through the grimy glass, making strange patterns of the sea.

'Wow, that was smashing,' she breathed. She had reached a rotting, green painted door, so she presumed that was the end of the adventure.

'You will open the door, please,' Eva snapped.

Pauline took hold of the handle and pushed and tugged until the door opened inward and swayed forward on a broken hinge. She caught it before it had gained any momentum and pushed it so that it flapped back against the glass wall.

'Good girl,' Eva called. 'Now you will see there is a platform. It is quite safe.'

Pauline walked through the doorway and found herself on a little balcony with an iron handrail around it. The blast of salty air seemed to feed her excitement and she ran across to look down at the sea.

There was a grinding scrunch beneath her feet and, suddenly, one of her legs was no longer there to support her. She grabbed wildly at the handrail and then looked down to see what had happened. Her leg was hanging through a huge, gaping hole and beneath her dangling foot, a rotten plank was plunging down towards the sea.

'I told you, you must not look down,' Eva barked.

Pauline came to her senses and pulled her leg back from open space. 'It's not safe,' she called. 'The planks are rotten.'

'Nonsense. It is the way you ran. You must always test the board in front of you. Now, help your sister.'

Weener started forward and Pauline instinctively held out her hand. 'Don't look down,' she warned, then seeing Weener had her eyes tightly closed, she snapped irritably, 'you can look at me, you fool.' Weener tottered forward, then grabbed the handrail and crowded close to her.

'That board might not be strong enough for both of you,'

Eva called. 'You had better climb the ladder; there by your side.'

Pauline looked round and saw that there was a ladder: an open, iron-rung ladder, climbing up the hangar for miles into the starry sky. She was about to say it was too dangerous, but the board creaked and moved ominously beneath her feet.

'Yikes!' Weener breathed urgently. 'Go on Pauline!' And she began to climb.

From the noise behind her, she could hear that the others were on the ladder. She made herself forget about the platform and she refused to wonder whether the iron on the hangar was as rotten as the wood. She looked only at the rung in front of her, automatically testing it to see that it was safe.

The wind was quite strong now. It thudded against her eardrums and made strange howling noises round her teeth.

'This isn't safe,' she called. 'I think we ought to go back.'

'You must not stop. We will all have an accident. Climb, you stupid girl.'

Pauline sighed and went on. Right at the top, there was a little glass-house. She tested the boarded floor carefully with her hands, then pulled herself up on it.

'It's safe this time,' she whispered to Weener as she pulled her up. Weener sat down beside her and rubbed her forehead with the flat of her hand.

'Don't just sit there, you lazy girls.' Eva's voice was closer than she had expected. 'Help your little sister.'

Pauline looked and saw Verity's yellow hair bobbing just below the platform. She reached down and pulled her over the edge.

'Now you must go on,' Eva ordered. 'It will not hold the four of us.'

'Do *I* have to?' Verity pleaded.

'Think of who you do it for, *Liebling*,' Eva murmured cryptically. Verity nodded and led the way out of the shelter.

The top of the hangar was a broad, square gallery which

stretched out right over the sea. The planks were rotten and whole patches of them were missing.

'Eva,' Pauline said after she had looked at them for some moments, 'this just isn't safe, you know.'

Eva nodded. 'Perhaps you are right. There is a safer way down. Over there, on the other side. Come on, it is not far to go.'

Pauline started forward, testing the planks with her foot. Wherever she found a rotten one, she kicked it out so that nobody would tread on it by accident. Where there was only one board missing, she could step over the gap quite easily, but two boards meant a jump and three were really frightening.

Weener came behind her, holding onto her hand every time she had to jump. Verity and Eva followed Weener, with Eva swinging Verity over the gaps.

It was very cold and the sea below them looked remote and terrifyingly far away. Pauline reached a gap of three boards, gathered herself together and jumped the open space. As she landed she felt the board move under her weight.

'Don't jump,' she shouted to Weener as she backed away.

'All English are cowards,' Eva sang teasingly and Weener bunched herself, then leapt at the rotten board. She landed with a dull thud. Pauline made a wild grab and caught her outstretched hands just as the wood disintegrated beneath Weener's feet. She pulled as hard as she could and suddenly Weener was in her arms. Pauline suddenly realized that her sister's life was infinitely precious and she found it impossible to let her go.

Eva swung Verity nonchalantly onto the board beyond them, then jumped across to join her.

'Listen, you fool,' Pauline shouted at her, 'we're not going any further. Got it?'

Eva put her hands on her hips. 'Oh yes? So you plan to stay all night, then?'

Pauline let go of Weener and sat down. 'If necessary,' she

said coldly. 'I'm not going to stand around while you murder my sisters. Sit down Weener,' she added, and Weener obeyed.

Eva eyed her with mock surprise, then looked down at Verity. 'Then we go on alone. You like it, don't you *Liebling*?'

Verity screwed her face into a worried frown. 'Not awfully,' she said. 'If it's all the same with you, Eva, I'd rather stay with the others.'

Eva shrugged. 'It is as I said. Cowards, all of you.' Then she turned and walked away, jumping the boards as if danger meant nothing to her.

'What on earth's got into her?' Weener asked.

'Search me.' Pauline looked along the platform. Eva had reached the end of the gallery and was waving a powerful torch at the sea. 'If you ask me, the woman's gone mad. Look at her. She's trying to light the sea up.'

Weener turned and started to giggle. 'Are we really going to stay here all night?' Verity asked anxiously. 'Are we, Pauline?'

Pauline sniffed and hunched her shoulders against the wind. 'We might as well have a bit of a rest.' She said it to give herself time to think, because it was obvious that she would never be able to get Verity back to the comparative safety of the ladder.

'Did you really ask Eva to bring us here?' Weener asked after a pause.

'Of course I didn't,' Pauline snapped. 'If I'd wanted to do it, I'd have done it on my own.'

Weener nodded. 'I didn't either. What about you, Vety?' Verity shook her head, then turned away from them and breathed frantically, 'Shh, she's coming back.'

'I don't care if she hears that we've found out what a stinking liar she is.'

Eva was quite close now and though Pauline spoke loudly enough for her to hear, she pretended not to notice.

'So,' she laughed, 'you do not move. You just sit like

154

frightened rabbits! German children would have enjoyed such a treat.'

They all stood up and this time Eva and Verity led the way back to the ladder.

'This time I go first, then you have a soft landing,' she laughed as she lowered herself onto the iron rungs. Verity followed her and, as soon as there was enough space, the other two started the descent.

It was not so bad going down, Pauline decided, but even so, she was very relieved when they reached the concrete base. This time I've really got you,' she told Eva angrily. 'You just wait till my mother hears about this. You could have killed us all.'

'And I shall tell the mother how you led your little sisters up the hangar in the night and how I, with great danger to myself, climbed up and saved you all.' She laughed triumphantly and clapped Weener on the shoulder. 'You ask this one who the mother will believe.'

Pauline immediately leapt to her own conclusions, and the reason for Eva's extraordinary behaviour became startlingly clear to her. Of course she had not minded putting them all in such danger: of course she had wanted to attract attention, and that was why she had been shining the torch. The whole operation had been arranged for one reason and one reason only: to get her, Pauline, into trouble. Her brain felt cold and clammy and she pushed her clenched fists deep into her pockets. Eva had bested her, but she would not give way to her rage out here. Like Eva, she would bide her time to take her revenge.

XX
The broomstick woman

Eva did not wake Verity on that morning after they had climbed the hangar, so she did not go as usual to the hut on the sand-dunes. She was quite relieved because she did not like the man who lived there. She and Eva had to make his smelly bed and sit in silence while he ate the food Eva had stolen from the nursery. Verity did not question the rights and wrongs of this daily ordeal. She knew only that she did it for the Führer.

Something very terrible had happened to Verity. She had grown up. She knew it must be so because she could remember nothing, and she felt nothing but an aching pain in the centre of her chest. Sometimes, fragments of pictures of the past would flash into her mind, but they were like snatches of a forgotten song heard through a window and, somehow, they always made the pain in her chest very much worse. She tried not to remember: she tried not to question. There were, after all, quite a few perks to being German. It was a pity she had to keep it a secret.

She did not play with her sisters any more because neither of them liked her. She did not play with the English children who came for the holidays because she spoke German so naturally now that she often forgot how to say things in English and that made them laugh at her. The German children would not play with her because she was too skinny and weak. Still, she consoled herself, she always had Eva and Eva loved her.

Verity had learned very little at school. She went because Pauline had said their mother would be sent to prison if they did not go regularly. Verity still loved her mother, but in a distant remote way like she loved God and the Führer. So she went to school and hated it. She hated the deference that was shown them, because it made her feel such a cheat. She hated the long boring mornings spent trying to read. She could recite the contents of the reading book and even, with great difficulty, write bits of it out on her slate, but she could not understand why the letters made the words.

Once again, she was grateful that she had Eva because Eva had taught her so much. She knew now that Hitler did not start the war. It was the Poles who were responsible, because they would not let Hitler build a railway in their corridor. They were stupid, so Hitler punished them which, in Verity's opinion, was more than reasonable. Eva was often unkind to her when she was stupid.

She had learned other things too: useful things like how to buy on the black market. You only had to get your hands on enough cigarettes and gin and you could have anything you wanted.

She had just bought herself a beautiful horse from the restaurant in the town. Verity loved horses, but she was not allowed to ride because she was too small. Sometimes, though, Eva took her down to the stables and the stable-boys would sit her on one of the horses and lead her around the cobbled yard. She loved the feeling between the horse and herself, as if they were having a private conversation which needed no words. The ride never lasted long enough and when she had been set down again, she would run her hand down the coarse, damp leg, feeling the tendons and muscles quiver beneath her fingers. Sometimes, if she was lucky, the horse would lower its great head and nuzzle words of love against her ear. Those visits to the stables helped the ache in her chest, but she was not allowed to ride, so her mother, as a compensation, gave her two bottles of gin and three hundred cigarettes to buy the horse in the restaurant.

It was a wonderful thing made of wood, and it was so cleverly balanced that it could walk. In the restaurant, it had beautiful trappings and lived on a mechanical see-saw so that it was perpetually in motion. Verity had imagined that the gin and cigarettes would buy the trappings and the see-saw too, but the man would only let her have the horse, so she had to improvise.

Everybody felt very ragged on that morning after they had climbed the hangar, so Eva said she would cover for them and they need not go on the treat that afternoon so long as they were good while she was out and promised not to quarrel. Verity promised earnestly: it meant she would have a whole afternoon to play with her horse.

Weener went downstairs to play ball in the grounds and Pauline disappeared into the linen-cupboard. Verity never questioned why she spent so much of her time in there, it was much too useful to have Pauline out of the way.

'Great news!' she told the horse as she lifted it out of the toy box. 'I have a wonderful treat for you. Today, you have a whole afternoon in which to enjoy yourself.'

She pulled Pauline's atlas out and made it into a see-saw with Weener's musical box. The horse clopped obediently backwards and forwards with Verity squealing with excitement every time it nearly toppled over the edge.

Outside, Weener's voice floated up as she called to the bouncing of the ball, 'Ollica bollica, *who's* a stollica? Ollica bollica, *nob*.'

The nursery was full of glancing light reflected from the sea, and Verity and her horse were happy. 'I'm on a see-saw,' she sang to it, 'you throw me up and you throw me down. I don't know whether I'm here or there.' They were the only words she knew of the song so she sang them again and again, louder and louder because the horse really seemed to like it.

Suddenly, the linen-cupboard door banged behind her. Verity felt her blood run cold as Pauline roared, 'For God's sake, stop that bloody row!' She froze as Pauline stomped towards her, because a corner of her mind knew there was nobody to save her from the inevitable attack.

158

'That's my bloody atlas.' Pauline ripped it away and the horse flew across the room, hitting the wall on the other side. Verity ran to it, but as she picked it up, the two front legs dropped off. 'My horse,' she wept. 'You've broken my horse.'

'Damn your bloody horse!' Pauline roared and hit her so hard she knocked her over. 'You stupid, stupid, stupid fool.' She punctuated each word with a kick.

Verity felt dazed and suddenly the world had gone silent as though somebody had switched off a radio in her brain. She was aware when Pauline stopped kicking. She was even aware when Pauline knelt down beside her and though she heard the words, 'Vety, Vety, I'm sorry. I didn't mean to. I'm sorry, really I am,' she could not take them in.

At last she knew what was wrong: nothing was real. She gathered the bits of her horse together and bunched them into the skirt of her frock. Then, with an incredible weariness, she walked out of the nursery, down the empty front stairs and around the building to the beach.

The light was dazzling, glinting off the sea to be reflected again from the windows of the *Offiziersheim*. It sparkled all around her, but it was not real. Weener was still playing ball, but her voice was not real. The only reality was the silence in Verity's head, the ache in her chest and the broken horse lying bunched up in the front of her skirt.

She stopped at the water's edge and looked down at the white bulge her big toe had made on the front of her sandal. There was sand on her shoes and it reminded her of something that had happened once, all that time ago when she was young. She had looked down at her shoes on a broad, earth path. 'They're all dusty,' she had said and somebody answered, 'That's not dust, darling. It's . . .' She could not recall what the last word was or who had said it to her. Now, she gazed at the glittering sea and longed to remember.

'Little girl. Little girl.' A voice floated across the sand and the silence.

Verity looked up. A broomstick woman was standing by the breakwater wearing a faded cotton frock.

'Little girl,' she called again.

Verity turned back to the sea. The woman was not real. She was only an echo in Verity's mind.

'Pollen.' That was what that voice had said all that time ago. 'That's not dust, darling. It's pollen.' She wished she could remember who had said it. It was somebody she had known who was very, very nice.

'Little girl.' The broomstick woman was beside her now. 'Do you know what time it is?'

Verity blinked and looked up at her.

'The time?' the woman demanded. '*Die* —' she looked lost for a moment then pointed to her wrist. '*Die* tick-tock?'

Verity shook her head in bewilderment and the woman tutted to herself. 'Are you English?' she asked.

Verity shook her head and then nodded vigorously.

'What have you got in your skirt?' the woman asked.

The pain in Verity's chest became so unbearable, she hardly noticed the tears gather in her eyes and roll down her cheeks. The broomstick woman brushed them aside with a rough spatula of a thumb.

'Oh, don't cry,' she breathed. 'I won't hurt you. What's the matter?'

Verity shaped her lips, but the words would not come. 'My horse,' she gasped at last.

'Your horse? What's happened to him, darling?'

'He's —' Verity began, but she could not remember the word. 'He's —'

'He's what?'

'Kaput. Kaput. Kaputzel.' She sobbed the last word out because she suddenly remembered the dog Kaputzel, and a picture of Goldie flashed into her mind. It was a terrible ingredient to her cocktail of misery. She let go of her skirt to cover her face with her hands. 'They hit him to death,' she wept. 'They hit him to death.'

'Oh darling,' the woman knelt down and surrounded her

160

with gaunt protection. 'Who beat your horse? Was it the Germans? Tell me. I'll see they're punished.'

'It was Goldie. They hit him till he was dead and I loved him.' Verity clung to the craggy neck and wept until the woman's hair was wet against her face.

'Where's your horse now?' she asked at last.

Verity paused, feeling suddenly stupid. 'Oh, he's not a real horse.' She pulled away and wiped the flat of her hand over her face. 'He's only a toy. I'm sorry, it was stupid to cry like that.'

The woman looked down and saw the horse lying between them on the sand. 'Is this him?' she asked as she picked him up. 'He's lovely, isn't he?'

Verity nodded.

'I'm sure we could mend him,' the woman went on. 'Would you like to come back to my rooms and we'll put him all back together again?'

Verity nodded again.

'Who was Goldie?' the woman asked as they walked together over the sand.

Verity sighed. 'He was my dog, but he died a long, long time ago.'

The woman patted her shoulder. 'We won't speak about him then. Sometimes it's best to forget.'

Verity took her hand and squeezed it because she entirely agreed. She wanted to say all sorts of things, but the woman's kindness was bringing her so close to tears again that she was almost grateful when she saw Eva hurrying towards them.

'Miss Verity. Miss Verity,' she called. 'Come here, you wicked girl.'

The woman stopped walking and looked down. 'Is that you?'

Verity nodded.

'Miss Verity, you wicked girl!' Eva shouted.

'We've heard you. There's no need to make so much noise, nanny.' the woman called and, though she stopped walking, she still held on to Verity's hand. Verity stood quietly beside her as Eva ran to catch them up.

Eva's face was red with exertion and there were broad, damp patches around the armpits of her dress. She stopped a little way short of them. 'Come here.' she ordered briefly.

Verity looked up at the woman and saw that she was glaring at Eva.

'Why do you say this child is wicked, nanny?' she asked in a voice which was so controlled that it was menacing.

Eva seemed confused. 'An expression, madam,' she murmured.

'You are not to use that expression. Do you hear me?'

Eva dropped a small curtsey. 'Yes madam, but Miss Verity must come. It is time for her tea.'

'Verity will be having tea with me today.'

'Oh madam, this is so sad. The mother has expressly asked that Miss Verity will have tea with her today. What shall I do? I am sure she will not know which one to choose.'

'She must have tea with her mother, of course,' the woman replied distantly, then she bent down and looked Verity full in the face. 'What would you like to do about your horse, darling?'

Verity looked back at her in confusion.

'Would you like me to take it with me now and mend it, or would you like to bring it round to me tomorrow?'

Verity gazed back, trying to understand.

'Well, answer the kind lady.' Eva told her.

The woman squeezed Verity's hand. 'Do you see that big building over there?'

Verity nodded.

'That's where I live. Now, my name is Aunty Gladys and I live in room 19. Do you think you can remember that?'

Verity nodded again.

'That's a good girl. Now, you bring your horse round tomorrow, and I'll fix him up for you as good as new.' She tried to hand the pieces back, but Verity pulled her hands away, shaking her head while she struggled to find the

162

words to express what she felt. 'Do you want me to take him and mend him, then?'

Tears of despair gathered in Verity's eyes. She wanted to say 'I don't know,' but the words would not come out.

'I think maybe I should take the toy.' Eva reached out for it, but Verity's voice suddenly worked.

'No,' she sobbed.

'All right.' The woman patted her head. 'I'll take him with me and mend him tonight. You can call round tomorrow morning. Just ask for Aunty Gladys in room 19.' She tucked the horse under her arm. 'Don't forget now, room 19,' she called when she had walked a little way across the beach.

'So,' Eva said mockingly after the woman was out of earshot, 'you give your precious toy to a mad woman. Sometimes I wonder whether you are German at all.'

Verity looked down at the sand as she trailed bleakly back to their quarters. She wished she could remember what she had rembered all that time ago, when she was standing by the sea.

XXI
The hut on the dunes

Verity felt edgy that evening as she and Eva set out for the hut on the dunes. It had been a lie about her mother wanting to have tea with the children, and that lie had cheated Verity out of her horse.

She could not define her feelings about Eva that evening. They veered sharply between blind obedience and bitter loathing. She went with her to the hut because she had to. It was vitally important that nobody should get suspicious because Eva was out on her own. They might follow her. They might even find the hut. But, on the other hand, if it had not been for Eva and her stupid friends, Verity would have been free to go round to Aunty Gladys at room 19 and demand her horse back.

She had not realized that Aunty Gladys was mad or she never would have let her take the horse. She hoped desperately that she would be able to get it back and she pushed all her anger with herself for parting with it into an unreasoning hatred for Eva, because she had not told her about Aunty Gladys's madness until it was too late.

Eva seemed to sense Verity's mood because she made no effort to talk as they walked along. Her lips were set into a tight line and her florid face was rigid with determination.

Looking at her out of the corner of her eye, Verity suddenly noticed how very fat Eva was becoming. Her body seemed to be made up of lumps and bulges which quivered and moved in separate directions as she struggled to keep up a good pace over the soft sand. Verity laughed inwardly and began to sing under her breath, 'I don't want her. You can have her. She's too fat for me. She's too fat, she's too fat, she's *too* fat for me.' It was a song the soldiers often sang as Eva went by. Usually, Eva took it in good part, but this time she stopped suddenly and took hold of Verity's shoulders.

'Tonight there must be no jokes,' she told her earnestly. 'Tonight you must be a good little girl.'

'Why?' Verity asked, with just a hint of rebellion in her voice.

'Because Otto is waiting for us at the hut. He does not like jokes. He does not like naughty children.'

Verity shuddered and tried to back away. Of all the things in her life, Otto was the most terrifying. It was Otto whom she and Weener had mistaken for Kurt's ghost and he had been frightening enough even in those days. But, though Verity had only met him once while they had been living on the island, it was enough to convince her that the reality of Otto was infinitely more blood-chilling than any ghost Weener could dream up.

'I want to go home.' she said as she struggled against Eva's grip.

Eva held on tightly. 'There is nothing to be frightened of. Otto likes you. "What a good little girl that Verity is," that's what he said to me when he met you. "I should like so much to be friends with her. What a pity that her sister screams every time she sees me. I should like to give sweets to Verity and take her for jolly treats, but what can I do when the sister is so stupid." That is what he said. That is what he thinks of you.'

Verity looked at her doubtfully. 'Did he really?' she asked, and when Eva nodded her confirmation, she went on, 'Weener isn't really stupid, you know. She only screams because she thinks Otto is a ghost.'

Eva snorted and took Verity by the hand. 'Your sister is as stupid as her name,' she remarked as they stomped forward again.

The hut was in the most deserted part of the sand-dunes. Even the sheep stayed away because the sand was very mobile and nothing could grow on it. The English and the local population never went there because there were so many unexploded mines. Only Otto, Eva and Verity knew their way through them.

From outside, the hut looked derelict and deserted. The windows had planks of wood nailed over them and it looked as if the door had been boarded up too. It was a trick, though. The nails had been cut through so that the door could be opened without disturbing the planks.

Eva went up to it and rapped out her special knock so that her friend would undo the fastenings on the other side and let them in.

Verity looked down at the sand as the door swung open, then she sidled in after Eva, wrinkling her nose against the smell. Though she and Eva cleaned the hut every day and often changed the bed linen, nothing would get rid of the frowsty stench of a human being living in close confinement, and the smell of the kerosene lamp which lit the dismal interior.

The hut was so small, there was only room for a bed, a chair and a table. Otto put the fastenings back on the door, then walked the little distance to perch nonchanlantly against the corner of the table.

Verity watched him with a horrible fascination until he became aware of the look and turned the full impact of his pale eyes on her. There was something very extraordinary about Otto's eyes and as he gazed at her, Verity defined what it was. They did not respond to outside stimulation. They reflected only what he was feeling and Verity was suddenly aware that he was enjoying the memory of the night he hit her on the head when she found him in the shower.

With difficulty, she turned away to look at Eva's other friend. He was sitting on the bed staring straight at her and Verity gasped with surprise.

'Why is he different?' she whispered to Eva.

'He is not different,' Eva snapped back.

'Yes he is,' Verity said indignantly. 'He's not the same

man at all. His hair's different. His face is different. His clothes are different.' She knew she should stop this endless inventory, but she felt impelled to go on because she was sure Eva was making a fool of her again. If the old friend had run away and a new one come in his place, Verity felt that Eva should own up to it, so she started up again. 'His hands are different. His shoes are different. His socks are —'.

The man stood up and the abruptness of his action silenced her. 'Get this filth out of here,' he barked at Eva.

Eva backed against the wooden wall. 'I have to bring her,' she stammered. 'I am the nursemaid. They would not let me come. They would suspect —'

The man slapped her face. 'I said, "Get this filth out of here".' His voice was measured and menacing.

Verity suddenly realized that by 'filth', he meant her. She backed away, feeling humiliated. She had an overwhelming need to escape from the violent atmosphere in the hut and, without realizing what she was doing, she fumbled the catches back and pushed her way out of the door.

'Now, you stay there and wait for me,' Eva called after her.

'I'm not filth. I'm not,' Verity shouted back. 'He's filthy and his bed stinks.'

Then, suddenly, she was running. Running from the hut. Running from Eva: from violence and the memories she could not remember. And above the sound her feet made in the soft sand, she heard her own voice sobbing, 'I'm not filth. I'm not. He's filthy and his bed stinks.'

Though the pulses in her head were hammering and her breath had to be gasped against the stitch in her side, she went on running and sobbing out her monologue until an outstretched arm broke her flight and a voice which sounded familiar said, 'Hey, hey, hey. Now, what's the matter with you?'

Verity looked up and saw that she was now very close to the *Offiziersheim*. Aunty Gladys was standing in front of her and, amazingly, Uncle Denis was at her side.

167

'This is the sand fairy I told you about,' Aunty Gladys murmured, and Verity was immediately reminded that she was mad. She rubbed her hand over her face, then sidled closer to Uncle Denis for protection. Uncle Denis bent down and looked straight into her face.

'Who's been upsetting you, Verity?' he asked, and his uncharacteristic seriousness took her by surprise. 'Was it your nanny?' he asked sharply, after a pause.

Verity shook her head.

'But somebody called you a nasty name. What was that name?'

'He said I was filth.' Verity squirmed at the memory and fought to stop herself from crying. 'I'm not, am I Uncle Denis? He's filthy and his bed stinks.'

'Who, Verity?'

'A horrible old man who lives on the sand-dunes. He lives in a hut and he's different today and when I asked why, he said I was filth.'

'Did your nanny take you there?'

Verity paused. At the very beginning, when she had begun to help Eva, she had sworn that if either of them was caught, she would never give Eva away.

'Well, did she?' Uncle Denis snapped, making Verity suddenly frightened of him. She shook her head. 'Then why did it take so long to answer?'

'I ran away.' A corner of Verity's mind was pleased with the lie because it was, after all, half true.

'But you've known this man for some time. You must have, or how would you know he was different?'

'I found him when I was playing. I felt sorry for him, so I gave him food.' She had rehearsed the statement with Eva so many times that it sounded convincing even in her own mind.

There was a pause and then Uncle Denis asked, 'Will you show me the hut?'

Verity shook her head. 'Why not?' The question came so fast that it nearly caught her off balance. She rallied in time and looked him straight in the eye.

'It's too dangerous,' she told him innocently. 'There are mines everywhere.'

'Ah,' he said knowingly, 'but you know your way, don't you, so it wouldn't be dangerous at all.'

Verity bit her lip. 'All right,' she said at last, 'but you must keep close to me. Any running around and, BOOOMPH, your head will be blown off.'

Uncle Denis nodded seriously, then turning to Aunty Gladys for the first time since the conversation had begun, he said, 'You'd better come too, Gladys. I'll need you to take Verity home when she's shown me the hut.'

The three of them set off in silence. Verity's mind was working furiously. She had never guessed that Uncle Denis would be clever enough to trap her like that and she wondered for the first time why he did not wear a uniform and why he drove around in a car instead of a jeep. It followed, of course, that he was not in the army, so perhaps it would not matter if she showed him the hut. As for Aunty Gladys, nobody would be likely to believe her because she was mad.

'Right.' Uncle Denis's voice cut through her thoughts. 'You can stop there, Verity. I've seen it.'

She turned and looked at him in surprise.

'I'm bigger than you. I can see over the dunes,' he explained.

'But what about the mines?'

He pointed to the trail of kicked-up sand which Verity had made when she ran away, then squatted down on his haunches. 'Anyway, I won't be moving from here till Aunty Gladys sends for reinforcements.'

Verity wavered but Aunty Gladys took her by the hand. 'Come on, darling.' For a mad woman she had a very kind voice. 'We're going back to my room to get your horse for you.'

Verity looked at her with relief and astonishment.

'He's all mended,' Aunty Gladys told her encouragingly.

'It was just that some of his strings had snapped.'

Verity squeezed her hand with gratitude and followed her happily back to room 19.

Eva was waiting in the nursery when Verity finally got home with her mended horse. She seemed friendly and she said nothing about Verity running away. Verity presumed she was not angry with her so she got ready for bed without telling Eva anything about Uncle Denis knowing where the hut was. She decided that Eva would probably never find out what she had done.

But that night, while Verity slept with the horse clasped in her arms, Eva came to her bedside and shook her roughly.

'You told them.' Her voice was a harsh whisper that rasped against Verity's ear.

'No,' she lied, clutching the horse more tightly.

'You lie. You told them. Open your eyes,' she ordered. Verity obeyed and saw that the sky outside the window was criss-crossed with searchlights like it had been whenever she peeped behind the blackout curtains during the war.

'What's happening?' she asked.

'They hunt for my friends. That's what is happening.'

Verity's heart lurched as she realized what she had done. 'I had to,' she sobbed more to herself than Eva. 'They made me. But I didn't tell about Otto or the Führer, honestly I didn't: only about the horrible man who said I was filth.'

Eva let go of Verity's shoulders, and hugging herself, she turned and looked at the searchlights playing against the window. 'You are a traitor,' she said flatly, 'a traitor. All your life you will remember how you betrayed.' And then she quietly left the room.

XXII
Going home

Verity and Weener were eating breakfast when Pauline came dancing out of the linen-cupboard.

'We're going home,' she sang. 'We're really going home. Verity's on a knife-edge and Mummy's had enough of Daddy. They've caught a stinking Nazi and we're going. We're really, really going home.'

Weener and Verity gazed at her in amazement while Eva, who was folding linen by the window, snorted.

'What nonsense,' she snapped. 'Sit down and eat your breakfast.'

Pauline put her hands on her hips and advanced menacingly towards Eva. 'I should be just a little bit careful if I were you,' she said tauntingly. 'Uncle Denis thinks you're probably a Nazi. He says you've done terrible things to Verity's mind and, at the least, you are a very wicked woman.' She walked back to the breakfast table and sat down. 'Funny,' she remarked casually, 'if anybody had bothered to ask me, I'd have told them just that.'

Eva gazed back at her. 'You will not be cheeky to me.' she said, but somehow, her voice had no conviction.

'Ha Ha.' Pauline shot her an evil look. 'Milk for breakfast! You really are frightened, aren't you?'

Eva snorted, then turning sharply on her heel, she flounced out of the room.

Weener chewed stolidly as she watched her leave. 'Really?' she asked as soon as they were alone.

Pauline nodded and helped herself to a cup of tea.

'When?'

Pauline looked up, her eyes bulging with excitement.

171

'That's the best bit. We're going today.'

Weener sniffed. 'Then it's a mistake. We can't go. Daddy's not here.'

Pauline took a swig of her tea. 'We're running away. You just wait. It's as true as I'm sitting here. I told you, Mummy's had enough of him.'

Verity looked from one to the other, trying to understand what was happening. She did not see how they could be going home when they were already at home, but she was too frightened of Pauline to ask her to explain.

She stood up and went through to the bedroom. The horse was lying on her freshly made bed and she picked it up, holding it close as she carried it over to the window. 'I'm on a see-saw,' she whispered into the wooden ear. 'You throw me up and you throw me —' her voice trailed away as she gazed through her tears at the sparkling sea. She did not know why the song made her so unhappy or why the pain in her chest was so unbearable today. 'You throw me,' she heard her voice whisper again in a broken monotone. 'You throw me. You throw me.'

She heard her mother come into the nursery and the noise of packing. She heard orders being given and her mother's voice saying with despair, 'No, Weener, you don't want to take that.'

'I do. I do,' Weener pleaded. 'It's my very best thing. Please Mummy.'

Verity heard it all, but she could not move away from the window or stop rocking the horse against the pain in her chest. Only when Eva's voice joined in the medley of noise did the spell break.

'Madam,' Verity heard her say. 'Madam, what do you do?' Verity ran to her and pressed her face against Eva's shiny black skirt. A protective hand closed over her head and she felt momentarily safe.

'We are leaving, Eva,' her mother's voice was cold and decisive. 'Verity, come here.'

Verity shook her head and pressed closer against Eva's

172

leg. Eva played for a moment with a strand of her hair and then she said, 'The Fräulein is ill, madam. It would be better to wait.'

'I don't think you understand me, Eva. You are dismissed.' Verity looked up incredulously, but her mother turned away. 'Do up the suitcase, Pauline.' she snapped. 'We're leaving right away.'

'Madam, I cannot let you do this. The father is away. The Fräulein is ill. I cannot let you.'

Verity never saw her mother turn. She moved so quickly that it happened in a split second. The air around her seemed to be vibrating with rage as she faced them.

'Stand away from my child, you Kraut.' Her voice was not loud, but it was so loaded with hatred that Eva backed away.

Verity tried to move with her, but her mother caught hold of her wrist. Without looking down, she snapped, 'Pass me the suitcase, Pauline. We're leaving now!'

The impetus of her anger was so strong that Verity never thought to take a last look at Eva. Clutching the horse, she bobbed obediently along beside her mother as they ran down the stairs. She did not look back at the *Offiziersheim* as the jeep pulled away. She did not look back at the island as the boat swept them across the sparkling North Sea.

The next two days were a long grey corridor of confusion and anxiety. Sometimes the corridor opened up into rooms which were customs posts. There were men in them: impossibly tall men who spoke no English. 'You have no papers, madam. You may not continue.' Sometimes they said it wearily; sometimes angrily, but her mother always retorted in exactly the same voice she had used to Eva, 'I do not speak your filthy language. Let me through at once!' and the men gave way.

It felt as though they were flying: as if they were running, although they were on trains and Verity knew that sooner or later they would all be caught and put in prison. Once she thought they would be caught for sure. A guard came into their carriage in the middle of the night and asked for their papers. Her mother looked stonily in front of her.

'Your papers, madam,' this time he said it in English.

'I have none.' her mother replied.

'Then I shall have to put you off the train. You may not continue without papers.'

'Do so, if you dare.' She stood up to threaten the guard and Verity suddenly saw how very small she was. There was a desperate courage in the tilt of her chin and her ramrod back. The guard wavered.

'How dare you come in here and harass us? How dare you threaten me?' she demanded.

The guard shrugged. 'Mad,' he muttered to himself in German as he backed out into the corridor. She slammed the door behind him, then turned to Verity. 'Go to sleep at once.' she ordered, and Verity screwed her eyes tightly shut.

The nightmare journey ended in a big, sunny room. They were in a port which looked exactly like Nordseeheim. Verity thought for a moment they had gone in a complete circle, until the woman at the desk began to speak in perfect English.

'Mrs Edwards,' she said. 'I'm afraid you can't go on. Not without papers. You'll have to wait while we contact your husband.'

Verity looked up at her mother, expecting another outburst of anger, but something had happened to kill her courage and she just stared blankly back at the woman.

'We can't wait!' Verity roared, because somebody had to keep the fight going. 'We can't! We're running away! We can't wait!'

'Verity,' her mother's voice was weary. 'Stop that stupid noise.'

'She's not really stupid,' Pauline confided to the woman. 'She's on a knife-edge, you know.'

Suddenly their mother began to laugh great shouts of laughter that sounded almost like a scream.

A woman in a blue uniform and a crisp white apron appeared from nowhere and ushered the children away. 'Come on,' she said. 'I've got a wonderful playroom that you're really going to love.'

Verity let herself be led away. She never thought to look back to see what was happening to her mother.

XXIII
Behind the red bars

It came as a shock to Verity to learn that their father actually owned them and that they could not even run away from him without his permission. This knowledge destroyed the last shreds of her affection for him so that when he finally caught up with them, she found it difficult even to be polite.

He was very subdued and spent most of the time talking quietly to their mother. It was almost as if he was afraid to test the level of estrangement from his children.

Pauline and Weener sat together on the boat which took them across the Channel. Verity sat just a little apart from them. She had made up her mind to keep her eyes closed unless it was absolutely necessary to see where she was going. She tried to pretend that Eva was sitting beside her, but it was a hard game to play because she could not remember what Eva looked like.

Nobody shouted at them in the customs-shed because they now had all the papers that anyone could want. They caught a train, then changed on to another which finally came to a halt in a terminus she was sure she remembered.

Outside, she broke her resolution and looked up at the faded letters over the facade. It said 'RITIS AILWAY' and she remembered that something very terrible had happened to that sign. It was broken and really should spell something completely different. She shrugged and followed her family to a waiting car.

'Hallo, girlies,' the driver called playfully as they climbed in, and when none of them answered, he added, 'Surely you haven't forgotten your Uncle Charley?'

They all shook their heads dutifully, although Verity was

sure they had never seen him before. He went on chattering and she closed her eyes to shut him out of her existence.

She quite enjoyed being in the car. It was so much smoother than the trains and she was disappointed when the engine stopped and her mother gently nudged her and said, 'Wake up, darling. We're home.'

· The car had stopped outside a house with a plum tree on either side of the gate. As Verity looked up at them, the pain in her chest suddenly exploded and she burst into floods of tears. 'It'll be all right, chicken,' her father said as he picked her up. 'You'll see. You'll have just as much fun at home.'

Verity ignored him because she was incapable of explaining that she was not crying because they had left Germany. She was crying because she had needed for so long to come home.

She slept from the moment she was put into bed. It was a deep, black sleep from which she never wanted to wake, and she bitterly resented it when Pauline and Weener stripped the covers from her bed. 'Get up,' Weener said excitedly. 'We're going behind the red bars.'

Verity obeyed automatically and the three of them tiptoed downstairs. 'Why do we have to be quiet?' she whispered after Pauline had closed the back door silently behind them.

Weener sighed wearily. 'Don't you remember anything?'

'I remember the plum trees,' Verity answered defensively, then glanced furtively at Pauline.

But Pauline was in too good a mood to be angry. 'Hurry up, you two,' she told them over her shoulder. 'I've got an important announcement to make.'

Weener and Verity followed her up the suburban road, across the green and through the red bars.

'Do you remember now?' Weener asked, and when Verity shook her head she added, 'Well, we all have to stick together. No running around.'

'Are there mines?' Verity asked, and her sisters shouted with laughter.

They crossed the tank-trap and walked through a field of long, wet grass. Verity could not think why the other two should want to come to such a dismal place. The sky was a uniform grey and she felt cold in her thin, summer frock.

'Fancy,' Pauline said importantly as she sat down on a crumbling wall. 'Fancy our secret society actually catching a Nazi.'

'Did we?' Weener asked incredulously.

Pauline nodded. 'It was mainly Verity's doing. I think we all ought to give her a vote of thanks. In fact, I don't see why we shouldn't make her honorary captain for today.'

Weener looked at Verity with admiration. 'How did you do it?' she asked.

Verity felt a lump rise in her throat and she squirmed away from her sister, fixing her attention on a dripping bramble that had crawled out of the thicket behind the ruined wall.

'What on earth are you crying for now?' Weener asked impatiently.

'I'm not.'

'Yes you are. Aren't you glad you caught a Nazi, then?'

Verity shook her head. 'I'm a traitor. I betrayed the Führer.'

'The what?'

'Crikey!' Pauline's voice was shocked. 'She means Hitler.'

'But Hitler's dead.'

'He's not!' Verity shouted angrily. 'He waits in the Black Forest and, one day when the time is right, he will arise and he will lead his glorious German people to their rightful destiny.'

Weener backed away from her and looked questioningly at Pauline. 'Well, you're not German.' Pauline said after a pause.

Verity nodded and turned back to the bramble. 'Yes I am.'

'Oh, don't be so stupid,' Pauline countered scornfully. 'I happen to remember you being born. You are very definitely English.'

'I'm not. Eva told me. I'm not English.'

Weener came up and put a hand on Verity's shoulder. 'Eva was always lying,' she said reprovingly. 'Honestly, Verity, I don't know how you could have believed all that rubbish. Don't you realize what she's done to you? She's made you betray your own country.'

Verity's feeling of guilt and confusion was suddenly so palpable that it was like a sister standing beside her, watching and disapproving. She shrugged away and from that different angle, she noticed something about the bramble which completely fascinated her.

'What are we going to do?' Weener asked Pauline.

'I vote that we forget everything that happened in Germany. I vote we never speak about it or speak German ever again. This could be very dangerous, you know. Verity is a traitor, of course. But it's England she's betrayed. We're going to have to cover up for her.'

Weener paused, then nodded. 'You could be right,' she said. 'After all, it isn't really her fault. What with her being so lonely and everyone being beastly to her, she couldn't really help believing Eva's rotten lies.'

'Yes,' Pauline's voice was thoughtful. 'And it is very difficult being a conquering hero, you know. She was really too young to be able to do it properly.'

But Verity took no notice of them. A spider was spinning a web between the bramble and the wall. It worked swiftly and deftly. And as Verity watched the web becoming ever more intricately beautiful, she made up her mind to mount guard and see that no flies got caught up in it.